ENDORSEMENTS

I can think of no one better than Dann Farrelly to write on such a crucial subject as the values of the Kingdom. Dann has been at the forefront of building a culture that reflects heaven in the context of both a local community and city. When we better understand the values of the Kingdom, we are more effective in creating a culture where healthy and impactful fruit grows. If you have a heart to see a Kingdom culture established, this book will help guide you on that journey.

Banning Liebscher
Lead Pastor of Jesus Culture, Sacramento CA

Dann Farrelly is a long-standing voice of trust and reason in what can only be described as a forest fire. His love for scripture and deep theological review have brought the flash points of revelational teaching into biblical accountability. As the Director of a school of ministry, Dann is flush with zealous students who want to make up a gospel that fits their experiences. While experiences are certainly a valuable part of life with a living God, all biblical core values, precepts, and frameworks will, in the end, support a solid theological tradition. *Kingdom Culture* is the sort of book that comes from years of doing just this. The process and discussion of many students presses on what we currently practice until they force us to represent what we are saying as teachers and leaders. This book will help you to both understand and present many of the supernatural themes and practices enjoyed at Bethel Church in Redding, CA. I highly recommend this book to anyone ready to better understand a supernatural culture.

Danny Silk
President of Loving on Purpose

For me, Dann is a hero. His love for God's truth to be accurately displayed has inspired me since the first day I met him. As an attendee of Bethel School of Supernatural Ministry (BSSM) I clearly remember Dann finishing every session and staying behind at the end to answer all our curios and often crazy questions about "what God meant when He said". . . in the Bible. I'm so thankful for the example I had and that Dann and the Bethel core team didn't allow their revelations to stop at just the learning level, but they took it where it belongs—into daily living! That is exactly what you get when you read this! You will discover where the nature of Jesus is demonstrated in you and also find powerful grace from the Holy Spirit to fill the areas you may sense lack in. Dann, thank you so much for your heart in this. I truly believe this God inspired book will set many free!

Ben Fitzgerald
Director of Awakening Europe
www.awakeningeurope.com

KINGDOM CULTURE

LIVING THE VALUES THAT DISCIPLE NATIONS

A CORE VALUES JOURNAL

DANN FARRELLY

DEDICATION

To my teachers and their teachers,
everything I know, I have learned from another.
To our students and their students,
and their students' students,
until His Kingdom is fully manifested.

KINGDOM CULTURE

LIVING THE VALUES THAT DISCIPLE NATIONS

ISBN: 978-1-64007-279-4

Published by Bethel Church
www.bethel.com

Cover design: Brianna Ailie
Interior design: Jonathan McGraw

Printed in the United States of America.

For additional information on Bethel School of Supernatural Ministry, visit our website:

WWW.BSSM.NET

TABLE OF CONTENTS

1 FOREWORD: BILL JOHNSON

3 FOREWORD: KRIS VALLOTTON

5 THANKS AND ACKNOWLEDGEMENTS

6 KINGDOM VALUES CREATE KINGDOM CULTURE

10 BETHEL STATEMENT OF FAITH

12 HOW TO USE THIS BOOK

15 **THE CORE VALUES OF BETHEL:**

17 GOD IS GOOD

33 SALVATION CREATES JOYFUL IDENTITY

49 RESPONSIVE TO GRACE

65 FOCUSED ON HIS PRESENCE

81 CREATING HEALTHY FAMILY

97 GOD'S WORD TRANSFORMS

113 GOD IS STILL SPEAKING

131 JESUS EMPOWERS SUPERNATURAL MINISTRY

147 HIS KINGDOM IS ADVANCING

163 FREE AND RESPONSIBLE

179 HONOR AFFIRMS VALUE

195 GENEROUS LIKE MY FATHER

213 HOPE IN A GLORIOUS CHURCH

229 KINGDOM CULTURE DECLARATION

230 NOTES

231 ABOUT THE AUTHOR

232 BETHEL SCHOOL OF SUPERNATURAL MINISTRY

240 ADDITIONAL RESOURCES

FOREWORD

Bill Johnson

Values shape culture, whether it's the culture of a home, business, nation, or church. Simply understanding the concept of culture, and its impact, reveals our potential for bringing a lasting and healthy influence to the world around us. It is an essential part of our service to our Lord Jesus Christ.

One of the most vital assignments we have in life is to discover and implement the values of heaven so that we can see God's will fully realized in our lives. Thus, we have been given this direction for prayer: *on earth as it is in Heaven*. Jesus gave this prayer to His disciples, and in it we find the backbone of our earthly assignment. Everything else—from the Great Commission to the Great Commandment—falls under the influence of this prayer's focused mandate.

Here at Bethel, in Redding, CA, we have been exploring what heaven's culture looks like for quite a while. We've realized that, if our discovery is genuine, its impact on us and others can be measured. In other words, the effects of heaven's culture on individuals, families, ministries, and all other aspects of city life must have outward, discernible significance to prove its authenticity. This is the purpose behind *Kingdom Culture*.

The author of *Kingdom Culture*, Dann Farrelly, is one of the greatest men I have ever met. We have worked together for over 20 years. His impact upon me, as well as our church family, is huge. I'm so thankful for him and his family, for his gift of wisdom and insight, and for his service to us. I believe he really is the most qualified of all of us to recognize, define, and write about what we've been exploring for all these years. He has done a masterful job in identifying and explaining the things that we have discovered in the Word, and all that we are learning to put into practice within the Bethel Church family. What we have discovered, to our surprise, is that when the culture we live is a true expression of the Kingdom of God, the Lord Himself lifts the veil of influence so that we might impact the world around us positively. He really does desire the Kingdom of God to be established on earth.

I am more excited for the release of this study, because of the subject matter alone, than I have been in a very long time. But, as I look through this manual, I realize that this is much more significant than even I originally thought. *Kingdom Culture* will be a game changer for many. Within each subject, the process of study has been thought through so intentionally. From the examination of scripture, to the measured impact on our thinking and lifestyles, to the activation of each lesson, this book has the capacity to impact the destinies of entire family lines. I don't think it's possible for anyone to go through this study and not be radically changed, inside and out.

This is a gold mine. For the glory of God, start digging!

Bill Johnson
Bethel Church, Redding, CA
Author of *When Heaven Invades Earth* and *God is Good*

FOREWORD

Kris Vallotton

Dann Farrelly has been one of my dearest friends since 1997, and I can honestly say that he has deeply processed and lived out the truths he presents in *Kingdom Culture - Living the Values that Disciple Nations.* He has chewed on these profound principles for years and has fruitfully expressed them in his everyday life, and now in this powerful book. Dann is an anointed teacher whom I trust and look up to. He has a wholehearted love for God's Word and a grace to help others comprehend and apply the truth of the Bible. Time and time again, I've seen him take complex revelation and translate it for our students at Bethel School of Supernatural Ministry. In this book, he releases a hunger for a deep-seated connection with the Word of God and a grace to understand the culture of God's Kingdom.

As humans, we are made to create culture. The way we process life, define relationships, communicate with others, treat family, lead, and think are all products of the cultures we come from, or the cultures we have worked to build around us. Culture is the result of lived-out behaviors that are driven through core values. Core values are the manifestation of the way that we view and experience life through our personhood. I can't think of a more effective way to express the Kingdom than to live out the culture of heaven on earth. One thing I love about this book is the clear way that Dann defines Kingdom Culture and unravels the intricacies of truth, never losing the power behind an idea but rather unfolding its potential. He presents core beliefs of our Bethel leadership in a way that you can grasp, hold onto, carry, and then give away to others. So much power lies in the sustainability of understanding God's Word in the depths of your being, to the point that it changes the lenses through which you see the world. This book is a catalyst for lasting personal transformation if you open yourself to the ways I believe God will speak to you through it.

Kingdom Culture - Living the Values that Disciple Nations was written in a way that enables you to process what you read and learn. God will meet you in its pages. Everyone who has ever been curious about the culture of Bethel, the truth about God's Kingdom practically coming to earth, or how to be a revivalist should start with the foundation of this book!

Kris Vallotton
Bethel Church, Redding, CA
Author of *The Supernatural Ways of Royalty* and *Destined to Win*

THANKS AND ACKNOWLEDGEMENTS

Not to be cliché, but it took a village to write this book: the Bethel Church village. This book is 20 years in the making. Most of these ideas did not originate with me. It is more accurate to say that I led a team who practiced and articulated what our senior leaders have been teaching. If I were to ask Bill Johnson and Kris Vallotton to write a foreword, I'd suggest they simply write, "Yes, I endorse all the concepts that Dann's team has collected which I have been teaching for the last two decades." Danny Silk could write the same sort of foreword.

The senior team of Bethel has lived in covenant friendship for more than 30 years. Bill and Beni Johnson, Kris and Kathy Vallotton, Danny and Sheri Silk, Stephen De Silva, Charlie Harper, Eric and Candace Johnson, Brian Johnson, Paul Manwaring, Banning Liebscher, and I worked out the values within these pages together as a team in real life. It has been a privilege to further articulate and shape what we have attempted to innovate and protect through this book.

Paul Manwaring, Irene Lopez, and Mark Brookes were instrumental as they realized that, taken together, these values were the essence of the culture we are attempting to pass on. Chris Cruz, Young Kim, Ben Armstrong, Matt Coil, and Katrina Stevenson, among others, graciously worked on the early versions of this book. It was a joy to refine each of the values and every supporting Bible verse with Dave Harvey, Bernie Ooley, Kristy Tillman, Darlene Edskerud, and Rich Schmidt. I feel as if they have carried me and this book over the finish line, for which I am deeply grateful.

KINGDOM VALUES CREATE KINGDOM CULTURE

The Lord made a universe, and on a particular planet in that universe, He created beings that were made in His image and gave them the honor of bringing their gifts and leadership to bear on His creation. God's direction to be fruitful, multiply, and fill the earth is not simply about more people wandering the planet, but rather about establishing a flourishing human culture. We were made and instructed to create society alongside the Creator. Humans are culture-making machines by design and this pleases God.

Everything we love about life existed in God before anything else was created. God is an eternal being who is, by nature, three persons, a co-equal culture of Holy Spirit, Son, and Father. There is a beautiful and dynamic society in the Triune God that He desires to see manifested on earth. In the death and resurrection of Jesus, God established freedom for believers from our broken human nature and broken culture. He gave His followers the Holy Spirit, restoring the desire and capacity to cooperate with God again. This means that part of God's salvation plan was the restoration of our original purpose: to once again thankfully and happily create Kingdom culture with God.

The Merriam-Webster dictionary says culture is "the set of shared attitudes, values, goals, and practices that characterize an institution or organization." Families, workplaces, neighborhoods, cities, and nations all have a culture. In fact, humans need the context provided by culture in order to understand themselves and thrive.

A healthy Kingdom culture enables people to live in peace, meaning, and prosperity, rightly connected to God and to one another. In Scripture, Christ gave us the foundations for a powerful culture, which we were meant to build upon for the sake of the world. By embracing the core values of Kingdom culture, it is possible to establish a powerful culture that thrives and heals diverse societies, and helps us to prioritize what we want to accomplish within the realms of society.

Every person has a worldview, full of values and behaviors, which orients them in a culture and organizes how they interpret and participate in the world. It is a continually developing inner explanation of reality, a story we believe and tell ourselves, which we've learned from our environment and culture. It answers big questions, like why we are here, what's really true, what happens after death, and so on. Part of what it means to be a disciple is having our inner story, or worldview, and our values brought into alignment with God's truth by the power of the Spirit. We read Scripture, pray, worship, listen to sermons, and journal for this very purpose: to perceive, think, feel, and act like He does as best we can.

Along with a worldview, there are also potentially thousands of other values running through the soul of every human being. Those representing our deepest convictions would be considered our core values. For instance, if one has a deeply-held conviction that God doesn't exist, this impacts values about miracles, responsibility, truth, and so on. On the contrary, if one believes God does exist and rewards those who seek Him, the whole direction and meaning of life changes. Core values are like the roots that nurture and sustain a large tree in a great forest, or the small seeds that become food-producing plants in a thriving ecosystem, or even like the foundation of a building that supports the structure, making it safe and sound and orienting it to the rest of the city. They are the deepest beliefs that direct our lives and when groups share the same values, culture is created.

However, core values are not just foundational and orienting; they're also filters, or lenses, by which we interpret experiences. If one believes God has bigger things to worry about, then a miraculous personal healing is simply remission, luck, or a mistaken prior diagnosis. If one believes at their core that God is an angry judge who causes everything to happen, then every natural disaster is a deserved punishment for some portion of the human race because, after all, everybody is guilty of something. Because of these filters, we see what we expect to see. A value is really at our core when it is the light by which we naturally see and interpret the world and it motivates our behavior. This can be experienced through something as simple as asking the Holy Spirit to help us notice the core values, or filters, through which we're interpreting the evening news.

Kris Vallotton of Bethel Church Redding highlights the distinction between aspirational values and functional values. In other words, those values that we aspire or hope to have versus those we truly possess which determine our behavior. For example, many think they have a high value for honoring others, but in practice only honor those they deem worthy. This means people of other religions, nationalities, denominations, or political parties receive little honor from them. As disciples of Christ, we're in a lifelong process of closing the gap between our aspirational core values and our functional core values. We will not be perfect at this, but Holy Spirit is patiently empowering and socializing us into Kingdom culture.

Over time, healthy core values reinforce a healthy identity and transform our personality in positive ways. The grumpy can become joyful, the frugal generous, and the fearful brave, until all the fruit of the Holy Spirit is manifested in us. Having accurate core values about life, self, and God lead to a good life and healthy communities.

At Bethel Church in Redding, a small city in northern California, we have been experimenting with the 13 core values in this book for over 20 years, attempting to live and apply them, as we ponder what it means to be a disciple and to disciple nations. As we *lived* these values, we experienced a shift in our connection with God and our role in bringing God's life-giving Kingdom to the world. We compiled this book after listening to and practicing what our senior leaders, Bill Johnson, Kris Vallotton, Danny Silk, Paul Manwaring, and others have been exploring and implementing together with our church family. These beliefs and practices are not the product of a brainstorming meeting. Rather, they are the teachings and applications God had given us, which were scattered throughout years of sermons, books, conferences, and worship songs. In this book, we have attempted to articulate what God has been emphasizing so we can reinforce and reproduce these values.

These principles are a work in progress, just as we are a work in progress. These convictions have deepened as we have interacted with believers and nonbelievers in many diverse and international cultures. We know that the 13 biblically-based core values that we are proposing cause life to thrive in any environment: a state penitentiary, house churches in predominantly Muslim countries, the buckle of America's Bible belt, a Canadian car dealership, a South African township, or Ivy League academia because we are watching it happen. We have been on a long journey and hopefully have distilled several timeless, universal, biblical core values that foster Kingdom culture.

The calling of our church is to expand God's Kingdom through His manifest presence. At our best, every service, sermon, staff meeting, worship set, and prayer time is focused on enjoying the Lord who dwells with His people and cooperating with His priorities. He is the prize. Everything else finds its proper place when God is central. These core values are not a formula. They only make sense within the context of God's presence. Applying principles without seeking His presence is like seeking a Kingdom without a king.

Each core value is powerful and motivational, and functions as a foundation and a filter on its own. However, when taken together, they create a way to think about and apply the Kingdom in any situation. Considered together, they create an ecosystem where life and identity in God can flourish. We have found them to be like a GPS map, highlighting where we are, when we are lost, where we should go, and how to get there. Working through them as a whole allows us to experience the balance they bring to each other, keeping each one from being distorted or oversimplified.

These 13 core values are not the final or only word on the Kingdom. There are many core values we don't address because they are common to Christianity and wonderfully expressed in a variety of ways by millions of Protestant, Catholic, and Orthodox believers. While they might not be expressly named, the essential teachings about love, obedience, faith, holiness, sacrifice, worship, and prayer are woven into these values.

These are not distinctives intended to separate Bethel from our brothers and sisters in the faith, nor are they the foundation of a new denomination. Rather, they are emphases the Lord has called us to steward. Other believers have been called by God to express the Kingdom differently then we have. We celebrate and need all expressions of the Kingdom. We may be shouting what others are called to whisper, while we are whispering what others are called to shout. Bethel is simply a small part of what our great God is doing and has been doing on the earth. He is big, beautiful, and complex just as people and culture are complex. It is no wonder that it takes a variety of ways to display His glory within the vastness of human experience.

One of the subtitles considered for this book was "Biblical Values that Disciple Nations" because these core values are based in Scripture and the applications we are proposing are consistent with God's Word. We encourage you to read the passages provided for each core value and see this for yourself. It is also important to note that these values are not our statement of faith. Rather, they flow from the statement of faith on the following page.

Building the Kingdom with the King is the most exciting, purpose-filled existence a human being can have. We are honored and excited to have you join us on this journey and hope this book will enable you to adopt, apply, and shape these core values to create your unique expression of the Kingdom in your life, community, and places of influence. When we consciously live in the presence of the Lord and have a foundational set of core values that we're practicing in community, we begin to develop biblically-based, Holy Spirit-led, life-giving strategies that create Kingdom culture and disciple the nations.

BETHEL STATEMENT OF FAITH

Our core values are properly understood within the context of our statement of faith; they do not stand on their own. They flow from our deep commitment to the Scripture, so we have included our faith statement here so you can appreciate that the gospel is the "core" of the core values we hold.

Bethel Statement of Faith
We believe...

...there is only one true God who is the eternal King, Creator and Redeemer of all that is. He is perfectly holy, just, loving and truthful. He has revealed Himself to be eternally self-existent - one being in three persons: God the Father, God the Son, and God the Holy Spirit.

...the Bible to be the inspired and only infallible and authoritative Word of God.

...humankind was created in the image of God to know and enjoy Him yet we willfully rejected the Lordship and glory of God for which we were intended. Because of this, sickness, death and judgment entered the world and now creation experiences the effects and consequences of sin.

...the Lord Jesus Christ, the one and only Son of God, was conceived of the Holy Spirit, born of the virgin Mary, and is God's Anointed One, empowered by the Holy Spirit to inaugurate God's Kingdom on earth. He was crucified for our sins, died, was buried, resurrected, ascended into heaven, and is now alive today in the presence of God the Father and in His people. He is "true God" and "true man."

...we are saved by God's grace, through faith in the person and work of Jesus Christ. Anyone can be restored to fellowship with God through repenting, believing and receiving Jesus as their Savior and Lord. The Holy Spirit convicts, regenerates, justifies, sanctifies and adopts us as we enter the Kingdom of God as His sons and daughters.

...in the ongoing sanctifying power of the Holy Spirit, by whose indwelling the Christian is enabled to live a holy life and minister supernaturally. The baptism of the Holy Spirit according to Acts 1:4-8 and 2:4 is poured out on believers that they might have God's power to be His witnesses.

...the victorious redemptive work of Christ on the cross provides freedom from the power of the enemy—sin, lies, sickness and torment.

...the Church consists of all who put their faith in Jesus Christ. He gave His church the ordinances of baptism and communion. The Church exists to carry on the ministry of Jesus Christ and further advance His Kingdom by undoing the works of the enemy, preaching and living the good news of God's love, discipling the nations, baptizing and teaching them to love and obey God.

...in the ever-increasing government of God and in the Blessed Hope, which is the glorious visible return of the Lord Jesus Christ to rule and reign with His overcoming bride—the church.

...heaven and hell are real places. There will be a resurrection of the saved and the lost, the one to everlasting life and the other to everlasting death.

HOW TO USE THIS BOOK

We hope this book will make you feel deeply loved by your Father who wants to teach His children how to see and think like He does. With this in mind, it is essential for you to have a listening heart and to talk to the Lord as you work through this journal. If you find yourself pursuing information and filling in blanks but missing connection with the Father, well then, you've missed the point. Changing and adapting truth at your core takes work, so ask the Holy Spirit to help you because He loves transforming and teaching us all things. This journal is not about self-focus or self-improvement. Being preoccupied with our own soul is not nearly as helpful as being preoccupied by what God has done for the world in Christ. He is the focus—the true core of any core value that is truly meaningful. Enjoy God's presence and have an ongoing conversation with Him as you take this journey of abiding with Him and embracing these truths.

Kingdom Culture: Living the Values that Disciple Nations will lay the foundation for igniting and sustaining personal and corporate revival. It's our hope this book stays with you for several years, that you'll work through it in a brief season but then return to it periodically to help these core values become the natural responses of your heart. This way, it will not only be a short term experience but also a life-long, personal reference that you author and develop with Holy Spirit.

This book can be used in a variety of ways: a 13-week personal devotional, a small group study with friends, a curriculum to lead a team or workplace into a Kingdom mindset, or to develop messages and talking points to encourage people around you to apply these values.

Each of the 13 core value chapters includes:

DEFINING THE CORE VALUE
Definitions of each core value, along with supporting scriptural references.

WHAT DOES THIS MEAN?
Further explanation and application of the core values.

DO NOT MISUNDERSTAND
Clarifying to avoid extremes and misinterpretation.

WHAT IS GOD SAYING TO ME?
Meditations on each definition and scripture, along with opportunities to respond to what God is saying to you.

ACTIVATIONS
Activities to help you partner with Holy Spirit to build each core value into your life.

TESTIMONIES
Space for you to capture testimonies to create faith to see God do it again!

MY MESSAGE
A message outline to help you organize your thoughts and revelations so you can communicate it to others.

HOW AM I DOING?
An opportunity for you to identify areas of strength and opportunities for growth.

GROWING IN THIS CORE VALUE
A place to set short- and long-term goals to help you take action and grow in each core value.

THE CORE VALUES OF BETHEL

IDENTITY

God is Good

Salvation Creates Joyful Identity

Responsive to Grace

DISCIPLESHIP

Focused on His Presence

Creating Healthy Family

God's Word Transforms

KINGDOM

God is Still Speaking

Jesus Empowers Supernatural Ministry

His Kingdom is Advancing

SERVICE

Free and Responsible

Honor Affirms Value

Generous like my Father

Hope in a Glorious Church

THE LORD IS GRACIOUS AND COMPASSIONATE, SLOW TO ANGER AND RICH IN LOVE. THE LORD IS GOOD TO ALL; HE HAS COMPASSION ON ALL HE HAS MADE.

PSALM 145:8-9 (NIV)

GOD IS GOOD

GOD IS GOOD

DEFINING THE CORE VALUE

God describes Himself as gracious and compassionate, slow to anger and abounding in love. God is good and, by nature, in a good mood.
Psalm 103:8–13; Acts 14:16-17; James 1:17–18; 2 Peter 3:9; Matthew 7:11; Galatians 5:22–23; Psalm 119:68; Zephaniah 3:17; Psalm 104; Exodus 34:5–7; Acts 17:22-31

The message, ministry, and sacrifice of Jesus perfectly reveal the nature of God as a good Father.
John 3:16–17; Hebrews 1:2–3; John 14:6–7; Isaiah 9:6; Colossians 1:19, 2:9; John 1:1, 18; 8:1–11, 19

God is a good Father; we can trust Him regardless of our circumstances.
Romans 8:28–32; Hebrews 11:6; Nahum 1:7; James 1:12–18; Matthew 10:29–31; Acts 16:23–26

Enemies come to steal and kill, but Jesus came to destroy demonic works and give us abundant life.
John 10:10–11; 1 John 3:8; Acts 10:38; 1 Peter 5:8–10; Ephesians 6:12; Mark 5:1–19

God's goodness is extravagant. As we remember and retell what He has done through our testimonies, faith is created that He is able and eager to do it again.
Romans 10:15-17; Hebrews 13:7-8; Acts 10:34-48; Revelation 19:10; Psalm 44:1-5, 119:11; Mark 5:18-21; Deuteronomy 6:17-24; I Chronicles 16:23–36; Joshua 4:1–9

WHAT DOES THIS MEAN?

God is for us; He chose to redeem us from our sin.
Romans 8:31–32; 5:8; I Corinthians 1:30; 2 Corinthians 5:19

God is not mad at us.
I Thessalonians 5:9; 2 Peter 3:9; John 10:10; Romans 2:4; Zephaniah 3:17; Romans 14:17–18

God's desire is to prosper us in every area of our lives: physically, mentally, spiritually, emotionally and vocationally.
Psalm 103:1–5; 2 Corinthians 9:8–10; Isaiah 26:3, 53:4–6; Luke 9:6, 56; Genesis 12:1–3; 3; John 1:2; Jeremiah 29:11

Jesus is our model. He healed all the sick He encountered and never said sickness was from God. In the New Covenant, God does not generally use sickness to teach lessons, build character or punish people.
Matthew 4:23, 8:2–3; Acts 10:38; Mark 3:20–27

We live with the practical conviction that God wants to save and heal everyone.
I Timothy 2:4; Ezekiel 33:11; Acts 10:38; Matthew 4:23–24, 8:1–3, 8:16–17, 9:35, 14:34–36; Mark 6:56; Luke 9:11

God will never take His purposes or His gifts from our life.
Romans 11:29; Ephesians 1:4–6; Romans 8:28–31

We are God's masterpieces. His process and pruning are always meant to reveal our true identity and release us into fullness of life.
Ephesians 2:10; Psalm 139:13–17; John 15:1–2; Hebrews 12:5–13

God hears and always responds to our prayers.
James 1:5, 11; Romans 8:26–27, 32; Matthew 7:7; 1 John 5:14–15; John 15:7; Luke 18:1–8; 2 Corinthians 1:20

DO NOT MISUNDERSTAND

We cannot do whatever we want and expect God to always bless us. God remains the ultimate judge of every human being.
1 John 1:5–7; Hebrews 10:26–27; 2 Timothy 2:19; Proverbs 8:13; Hebrews 9:27; 2 Corinthians 5:10; Galatians 5:13–24

God is hurt by our sinful actions and will lovingly confront us if and when we sin.
Hebrews 12:7–11; Ephesians 4:17–32; Isaiah 65:2

Despite God's goodness and love, some people will still choose hell over heaven.
John 3:17–18; Romans 1:20–23, 8:1–8; Matthew 7:21–23

The life of a believer is not free from trials or persecution.
2 Timothy 3:12; John 16:33; Romans 8:31–39; Philippians 3:10; Psalm 34:19; James 1:2–4

Every believer is responsible for stewarding and growing the gifts and talents God has given us.
Matthew 25:14–30; 2 Timothy 1:6; 1 Corinthians 9:24–27; Philippians 3:12–14

In His goodness, God doesn't always respond to our prayers in the way or timing we expect.
2 Peter 3:9; Isaiah 55:8–9; Luke 18:1–8; Philippians 4:6–7

Write one or two of your own "What Does This Mean?" statements for *God is Good*, along with one or two supporting Scriptures.

-
-

Try to think of one or two more ways the core value *God is Good* could potentially be misunderstood, along with one or two Scriptures to correct these misunderstandings.

-
-

WHAT IS GOD SAYING TO ME?

As you read each of the five core value definitions and supporting scriptures below, take time to wait quietly with the Lord, asking Him, *"What are You saying to me about this core value?"* Use the space below each definition to journal what comes to your mind and spirit as you listen: thoughts, impressions, Scriptures, pictures, etc...

God describes Himself as gracious and compassionate, slow to anger and abounding in love. God is good and, by nature, in a good mood.
Acts 14:16-17; James 1:17–18; 2 Peter 3:9; Matthew 7:11; Galatians 5:22–23; Psalm 119:68; Zephaniah 3:17; Psalm 104; Exodus 34:5–7; Acts 17:22-31

"The Lord is compassionate and gracious, slow to anger and abounding in lovingkindness. He will not always strive with us, nor will He keep His anger forever. He has not dealt with us according to our sins, nor rewarded us according to our iniquities. For as high as the heavens are above the earth, so great is His lovingkindness toward those who fear Him. As far as the east is from the west, so far has He removed our transgressions from us. Just as a father has compassion on his children, so the Lord has compassion on those who fear Him." - Psalm 103:8–13

The message, ministry, and sacrifice of Jesus perfectly reveal the nature of God as a good Father.
John 14:6–7; Isaiah 9:6; Colossians 1:19, 2:9; John 1:1, 18; 8:1–11, 19

"For God so loved the world, that He gave His only begotten Son, that whoever believes in Him shall not perish, but have eternal life. For God did not send the Son into the world to judge the world, but that the world might be saved through Him." - John 3:16–17

"In these last days God has spoken to us in His Son, whom He appointed heir of all things, through whom also He made the world. And He is the radiance of His glory and the exact representation of His nature, and upholds all things by the word of His power. When He had made purification of sins, He sat down at the right hand of the Majesty on high." - Hebrews 1:2–3

G

God is a good Father; we can trust Him regardless of our circumstances.
Hebrews 11:6; Nahum 1:7; James 1:12–18; Matthew 10:29–31; Acts 16:23–26

"And we know that God causes all things to work together for good to those who love God, to those who are called according to His purpose. For those whom He foreknew, He also predestined to become conformed to the image of His Son, so that He would be the firstborn among many brethren; and these whom He predestined, He also called; and these whom He called, He also justified; and these whom He justified, He also glorified. What then shall we say to these things? If God is for us, who is against us? He who did not spare His own Son, but delivered Him over for us all, how will He not also with Him freely give us all things?" - Romans 8:28–32

Enemies come to steal and kill, but Jesus came to destroy demonic works and give us abundant life.
Acts 10:38; 1 Peter 5:8–10; Ephesians 6:12; Mark 5:1–19

"The thief comes only to steal and kill and destroy; I came that they may have life, and have it abundantly. I am the good shepherd; the good shepherd lays down His life for the sheep." - John 10:10–11

"The one who practices sin is of the devil; for the devil has sinned from the beginning. The Son of God appeared for this purpose, to destroy the works of the devil." - 1 John 3:8

God's goodness is extravagant. As we remember and retell what He has done through our testimonies, faith is created that He is able and eager to do it again.
Acts 10:34-48; Revelation 19:10; Psalm 44:1-5, 119:11; Mark 5:18-21; Deuteronomy 6:17-24;
I Chronicles 16:23–36; Joshua 4:1–9

"And how can anyone preach unless they are sent? As it is written: 'How beautiful are the feet of those who bring good news!' But not all the Israelites accepted the good news. For Isaiah says, 'Lord, who has believed our message?' Consequently, faith comes from hearing the message, and the message is heard through the word about Christ." - Romans 10:15-17

"Remember your leaders, who spoke the word of God to you. Consider the outcome of their way of life and imitate their faith. Jesus Christ is the same yesterday and today and forever." - Hebrews 13:7-8

ACTIVATIONS

As you have been studying and meditating on this core value, how has it changed your perspective of God? Take a few minutes to write a short list of how you viewed God *before* exploring this core value and how you view God now.

Before studying this core value, I saw God as...

After studying this core value, I now see God as...

Ask two friends or family members to tell you personal stories that display God's goodness in their lives. Write down which aspects of God's goodness you admire in each of the testimonies. For example: *"I love how creative God is in this testimony. He doesn't wait until we are perfect to intervene."*

-
-

G

TESTIMONIES

"He really is good. Eight years ago my wife and I were starting over. After six years on the mission field, we came back to the States with only four suitcases to our name. As we found our way to Bethel, God directed me to attend Bethel School of Supernatural Ministry. With Bible college and six years of successful ministry under my belt, this felt like ten steps backwards. Along with that, the only job I could get was working part time at a pet shop stocking shelves. Two years and five jobs later I was in an environment of miracles but felt crippled with discouragement. In desperation, I revisited a place of victory in my past called 'thankfulness.' As I daily turned my affections to what I was thankful for, I started to live from a place of worship. I found myself blessing the people who would be sitting on the toilets I was cleaning and I started believing it was impossible for me to not experience God's goodness both now and in the next season of my life. It was as if a floodgate of God's goodness opened over my life. The next year I got my dream job, paid off debts, received gifts of money, and we purchased our first house. Yeah! He really is that good! I have learned to live from God's goodness and focus on what He is doing."

-MATT C.

Write one or two stories of times you saw the goodness of God in your life.

•

•

MY MESSAGE

Whether preaching from a pulpit or talking with friends at a coffee shop, use this sermon preparation guide to organize your thoughts so you can help others understand that God is good.

My favorite scriptures for this core value:

My interpretation of these scriptures:

Key points I want to communicate:

The key phrase of the testimony I'll share as an example of this core value:

Example of how these truths could be applied to a real life situation:

The change, inspiration, impartation and/or call to action I want others to embrace after learning that God is good:

G

HOW AM I DOING?

Take a few minutes to reread the core value definitions at the beginning of this chapter and then rate yourself from 1–5 in each area below to help you identify strengths and opportunities for growth. Use this information to create personal growth goals on the following page.

1 / NEVER **2** / RARELY **3** / SOMETIMES **4** / OFTEN **5** / ALWAYS

I KNOW GOD IS GOOD

____ I can articulate it.

____ I can identify it in Scripture, books, movies, testimonies, sermons, and life.

____ I have experienced it in personal and/or corporate settings.

I DO THIS CORE VALUE

____ I am taking risks and sharing testimonies as I practice this core value.

____ I invite people into my life who exhibit, call out and give me feedback in this area.

I BELIEVE GOD IS GOOD

____ I have identified and replaced opposing beliefs and behaviors that hinder my growth in this area.

____ I believe it even when I am alone and no one is watching.

____ My level of hope and expectation has increased in this area.

____ I usually view and respond to life through the lens of this truth.

I REPRODUCE GOD IS GOOD

____ I carry the strength of it as I serve others and build community.

____ I am intentional in reproducing it in others and can see their progress.

____ I have stories of how others have recognized and been impacted by it in my life.

I AM THIS CORE VALUE

____ I have consistently lived each of the prior stages for many years in a variety of settings.

____ It is my natural response as I make decisions and respond to situations in my everyday life.

____ I naturally multiply it. I can identify people whom I have taught who are now effectively teaching others to live this core value.

GROWING IN THIS CORE VALUE

Using your personal assessment from the previous page, ask Holy Spirit to help you write a short-term and long-term goal for the following areas. Remember to make your goals time-specific, measurable, and realistic. Choose one to focus on this week and, as you accomplish it, come back and check it off so you can see your growth. Below are some examples to get you started.

MYSELF

- ☐ For the next seven days, instead of being stressed or anxious when something goes wrong, I will say Romans 8:28 aloud over my life and circumstances.
- ☐ Short-range goal: ______
- ☐ Long-range goal: ______

MY HOME/FAMILY

- ☐ I will intentionally look for three opportunities to reproduce the truth of God's goodness with my children/roommates this week.
- ☐ Short-range goal: ______
- ☐ Long-range goal: ______

MY PLACE OF WORK/SCHOOL

- ☐ By the end of the week, I will retell two stories of God's goodness to three or more of my coworkers/classmates.
- ☐ Short-range goal: ______
- ☐ Long-range goal: ______

OTHER

- ☐ ______
- ☐ ______

NOTES

G

G

WE DON'T

WORK *FOR* THE

LOVE OF GOD,

WE WORK

FROM HIS LOVE.

KRIS VALLOTTON

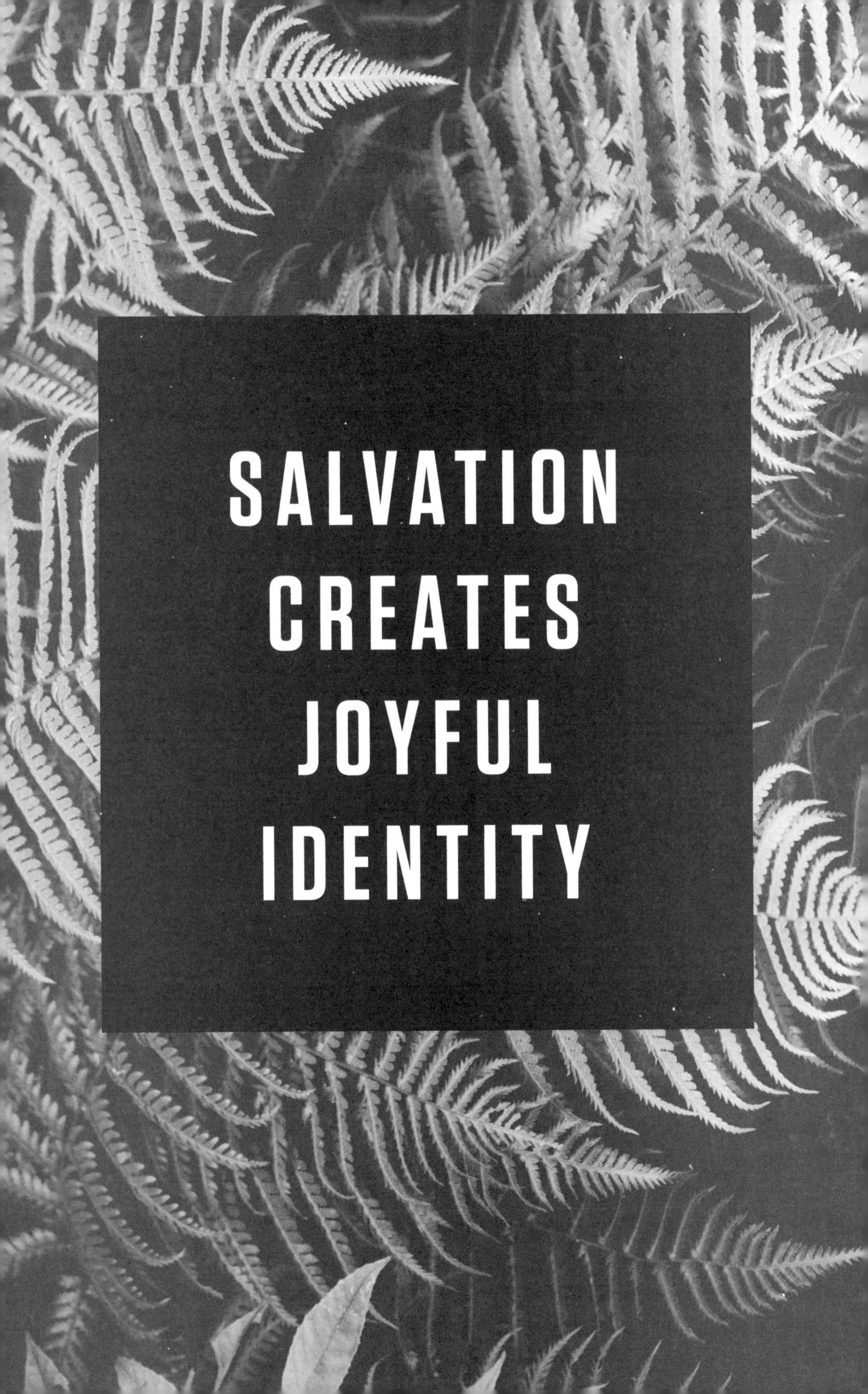
SALVATION
CREATES
JOYFUL
IDENTITY

SALVATION CREATES JOYFUL IDENTITY

DEFINING THE CORE VALUE

Jesus has won absolute victory! We are forgiven and freed from the enemy's power of sin, sickness, lies, and torment. Now we live in the power of righteousness, healing, truth, and joy!
Romans 8:1–4; 2 Corinthians 5:17; Romans 6:4; Galatians 2:20; Hebrews 2:14–15; Galatians 5:22–24; 1 Corinthians 15:56–57; Revelation 1:12–18

We are adopted as royalty into God's family and commanded to help others be reconciled with the Father and come home.
Romans 8:14–17; John 1:12; 2 Corinthians 5:18–21; 1 Peter 2:9; 1 John 3:1; Luke 15:11–32

We are simultaneously joyful servants, trusted friends, and beloved children of our Lord.
John 15:12–15; Psalm 16:11; Hebrews 1:9, 12:2; Matthew 25:23; Psalm 100:2; Galatians 1:10; Matthew 23:11–12; John 1:12; 1 John 3:1; Matthew 25:14–30

We are new creations, not merely sinners saved by grace but saints who have been given His righteousness so we can partner with our Father God.
2 Corinthians 5:17–21; 1 Corinthians 1:30; Romans 3:21–26, 8:1, 30; Galatians 2:19–20; Acts 26

WHAT DOES THIS MEAN?

S

We become new creations when we are born again in Christ. When we resist sin, we are not fighting against our old nature but instead we are cooperating with our new selves in Him. We are both sanctified and embracing sanctification. We are not working for victory, but rather from His victory.
Ephesians 2:4–6; Romans 3:24, 8:1–4, 29–30, 33–34; Galatians 2:20; 1 John 4:17

We no longer live under shame or condemnation because it has been lifted off of us by His grace.
Romans 8:1; John 3:17

Freedom, blessing, and abundant life are available to us now.
John 10:10; 3 John 2; 2 Corinthians 9:8–11; Matthew 6:33; Mark 10:29–30; Proverbs 3:9–10; Philippians 4:19

God doesn't remember our sins nor does He hold them against us, therefore we are not defined by our past.
Isaiah 43:25; Psalm 103:12; Micah 7:19; Romans 6:4, 8:1–2; Hebrews 9:26; 1 John 1:9; Acts 3:19; 2 Corinthians 5:17

We have been given authority and access to God's resources for the sake of the world.
Matthew 18:18–19; Luke 9:1–2, 10:1, 19; Matthew 28:18–19; John 14:12–14; Ephesians 2:10; Acts 10:37–38; Luke 15:31

We are citizens of another Kingdom and live from heaven towards earth.
Philippians 3:20; Ephesians 2:4–7, 19; 1 Peter 2:9; 1 John 4:17; Colossians 1:13, 3:1–3

Our new normal is to hunger and thirst for His righteousness to be revealed in the earth.
Matthew 5:6, 6:33; Acts 2:42–47; Philippians 4:8

One way to renew our minds and establish new habits of the heart and mind is by believing and declaring His truth and promises.
Romans 12:2; 2 Corinthians 1:20–22; Ephesians 4:21–24; John 8:31–32; Job 22:28

We can grow in our ministry and gifts through the laying on of hands and receiving impartation from other believers.
Matthew 10:41; Acts 13:2–3; 1 Timothy 4:14; 2 Timothy 1:6; Romans 1:11–12

DO NOT MISUNDERSTAND

Even though we are royalty in Christ, we still serve wholeheartedly because we follow the Servant-King!
John 13:13–17; Matthew 20:28; Mark 9:35, 10:42–45

Although each of us is made holy in Christ, we are all still in the process of growing into His fullness as we seek after Him.
Philippians 3:12–15; Matthew 6:32–33; Romans 12:2; 2 Corinthians 3:17–18

Sin has consequences. We take it seriously because God takes it seriously. We take responsibility for our sin and are quick to repent and reconcile with those that our sin has affected.
James 5:16; 1 John 1:7–9, 2:1–2; Acts 5:1–11

We may not always do whatever we want because our actions affect our relationship with God and His plans in this world.
Galatians 5:13–26; 1 Corinthians 6:18–20; Ephesians 5:15–21; Romans 6:1–2; 1 Corinthians 8:9

We feel godly conviction when we sin.
2 Corinthians 7:9–10; Romans 6:1–2; Luke 19:8–10; Psalm 51

We are not Jesus; Jesus is God the Son, distinct from creation.
Hebrews 1:1–3; Colossians 1:15–20, 2:9–12; John 5:19–27; Matthew 24:4–5

S

Write one or two of your own "What Does This Mean?" statements for *Salvation Creates Joyful Identity*, along with one or two supporting Scriptures.

-
-

Try to think of one or two other ways the core value *Salvation Creates Joyful Identity* could potentially be misunderstood, along with one or two Scriptures to correct these misunderstandings.

-
-

WHAT IS GOD SAYING TO ME?

As you read each of the four core value definitions and supporting scriptures below, take time to wait quietly with the Lord, asking Him, *"What are You saying to me about this core value?"* Use the space below each definition to journal what comes to your mind and spirit as you listen: thoughts, impressions, Scriptures, pictures, etc...

Jesus has won absolute victory! We are forgiven and freed from the enemy's power of sin, sickness, lies, and torment. Now we live in the power of righteousness, healing, truth, and joy!
2 Corinthians 5:17; Romans 6:4; Galatians 2:20; Hebrews 2:14–15; Galatians 5:22–24; 1 Corinthians 15:56–57; Revelation 1:12–18

"Therefore there is now no condemnation for those who are in Christ Jesus. For the law of the Spirit of life in Christ Jesus has set you free from the law of sin and of death. For what the Law could not do, weak as it was through the flesh, God did: sending His own Son in the likeness of sinful flesh and as an offering for sin, He condemned sin in the flesh, so that the requirement of the Law might be fulfilled in us, who do not walk according to the flesh but according to the Spirit." - Romans 8:1–4

We are adopted as royalty into God's family and commanded to help others be reconciled with the Father and come home.
John 1:12; 2 Corinthians 5:18–21; 1 Peter 2:9; 1 John 3:1; Luke 15:11–32

"For all who are being led by the Spirit of God, these are sons of God. For you have not received a spirit of slavery leading to fear again, but you have received a spirit of adoption as sons by which we cry out, 'Abba! Father!' The Spirit Himself testifies with our spirit that we are children of God, and if children, heirs also, heirs of God and fellow heirs with Christ, if indeed we suffer with Him so that we may also be glorified with Him." - Romans 8:14–17

We are simultaneously joyful servants, trusted friends, and beloved children of our Lord.
Psalm 16:11; Hebrews 1:9, 12:2; Matthew 25:23; Psalm 100:2; Galatians 1:10; Matthew 23:11–12; John 1:12; 1 John 3:1; Matthew 25:14–30

S

"This is My commandment, that you love one another, just as I have loved you. Greater love has no one than this, that one lay down his life for his friends. You are My friends if you do what I command you. No longer do I call you slaves, for the slave does not know what his master is doing; but I have called you friends, for all things that I have heard from My Father I have made known to you." - John 15:12–15

We are new creations, not merely sinners saved by grace but saints who have been given His righteousness so we can partner with our Father God.
1 Corinthians 1:30; Romans 3:21–26, 8:1, 30; Galatians 2:19–20; Acts 26

"Therefore if anyone is in Christ, he is a new creature; the old things passed away; behold, new things have come. Now all these things are from God, who reconciled us to Himself through Christ and gave us the ministry of reconciliation, namely, that God was in Christ reconciling the world to Himself, not counting their trespasses against them, and He has committed to us the word of reconciliation. Therefore, we are ambassadors for Christ, as though God were making an appeal through us; we beg you on behalf of Christ, be reconciled to God. He made Him who knew no sin to be sin on our behalf, so that we might become the righteousness of God in Him." - 2 Corinthians 5:17–21

ACTIVATIONS

Find a place where you can be alone. Turn on worship music, close your eyes, and ask the Holy Spirit to show you the Father. Imagine yourself sitting on His lap and leaning your head against His chest. Ask Him what He thinks and feels about you. Ask Him how He describes you, such as what names He calls you and why. In the space below draw or write down the words, pictures and phrases Father God shows you about your identity. How do you feel about what you saw or heard? How do these things change the way you see yourself?

Write five statements about who you are and who you are becoming and/or want to become as a new creation in Christ and in your royal identity. For example, *I love laughing and laugh all the time; joy is my strength; I prosper in all my relationships; I consistently bring God encounters to other people; I am full of hope,* etc. Declare your statements aloud twice a day for a week and take notice of how your thoughts and behaviors change.

-
-
-
-
-

TESTIMONIES

"Throughout high school, I was lukewarm in my faith, unsure of who I was, and trying to find myself through social status. When I was 17, I went to a revival meeting in Brownsville, Florida and ended up at the front of the church crying with a friend for 20 minutes as we repented and dedicated our whole lives to Jesus. After that, a supernatural joy came over me and I literally could not stop laughing for two days and nights. God showed me joy comes to those who surrender their lives to Jesus and that the covenant we receive from Him is abundant life. This abundant life destroys depression, hurt, and anxiety and we get to live from this place for the rest of our lives, not just for a moment. My life was never the same after that and I started to see revival spreading all around me. I learned salvation and joy are not just events, but rather a way of life that gives us both security in our identity and abundant life."

-CHAD D.

Write two stories of how Jesus transformed your identity or that of someone you know.

-
-

MY MESSAGE

Whether preaching in a Sunday school classroom or talking with friends in the break room, use this sermon preparation guide to organize your thoughts so you can help others understand that salvation creates joyful identity.

My favorite scriptures for this core value:

My interpretation of these scriptures:

Key points I want to communicate:

The key phrase of the testimony I'll share as an example of this core value:

Give an example of how these truths could be applied to a real life situation:

What change, inspiration, impartation, and/or call to action do I want others to embrace after learning that salvation creates joyful identity?

HOW AM I DOING?

Take a few minutes to reread the core value definitions at the beginning of this chapter and then rate yourself from 1-5 in each area below to help you identify strengths and opportunities for growth. Use this information to help you create personal growth goals on the following page.

1 / NEVER **2** / RARELY **3** / SOMETIMES **4** / OFTEN **5** / ALWAYS

I KNOW SALVATION CREATES JOYFUL IDENTITY

____ I can articulate it.

____ I can identify it in Scripture, books, movies, testimonies, sermons, and life.

____ I have experienced it in personal and/or corporate settings.

I DO THIS CORE VALUE

____ I am taking risks and sharing testimonies as I practice this core value.

____ I invite people into my life who exhibit, call out and give me feedback in this area.

I BELIEVE SALVATION CREATES JOYFUL IDENTITY

____ I have identified and replaced opposing beliefs and behaviors that hinder my growth in this area.

____ I believe it even when I am alone and no one is watching.

____ My level of hope and expectation has increased in this area.

I REPRODUCE SALVATION CREATES JOYFUL IDENTITY

____ I carry the strength of it as I serve others and build community.

____ I am intentional in reproducing it in others and can see their progress.

____ I have stories of how others have recognized and been impacted by it in my life.

I AM THIS CORE VALUE

____ I have consistently lived each of the prior stages for many years in a variety of settings.

____ It is my natural response as I make decisions and respond to situations in my everyday life.

____ I am an innovator, explorer, and articulator of it and people seek my wisdom concerning it.

GROWING IN THIS CORE VALUE

Using your personal assessment from the previous page, ask Holy Spirit to help you write a short-term and long-term goal for the following areas. Remember to make your goals time-specific, measurable, and realistic. Choose one to focus on this week and, as you accomplish it, come back and check it off so you can see your growth. Below are some examples to get you started.

MYSELF

- [ ] For the next seven days, I will look for this core value in at least four different places in my everyday life, such as the Bible, books, movies, songs, testimonies, sermons, etc...
- [ ] Short-range goal: ______________________
- [ ] Long-range goal: ______________________

MY HOME/FAMILY

- [ ] I will set aside one hour this week to create a picture, song, or poem that shows my new identity in Christ.
- [ ] Short-range goal: ______________________
- [ ] Long-range goal: ______________________

MY PLACE OF WORK/SCHOOL

- [ ] Over this next week, I will look for someone who exhibits this core value at work/school and ask them to help me grow in it by giving me feedback on how well I am living it.
- [ ] Short-range goal: ______________________
- [ ] Long-range goal: ______________________

OTHER

- [ ] ______________________
- [ ] ______________________

NOTES

S

S

IF YOU BELIEVE

IN GRACE, THEN

LET IT CHANGE YOU.

DO NOT USE IT AS

AN EXCUSE TO STAY

THE WAY YOU ARE.

JOYCE MEYER

RESPONSIVE TO GRACE

RESPONSIVE TO GRACE

DEFINING THE CORE VALUE

We joyfully experience the astounding, undeserved love of God and His ongoing power to transform us. His transforming love and power are inseparable from one another.
John 3:16–17; Ephesians 1:4–5, 2:8–10; Romans 5:6–11; Mark 5:1–20

God scandalously loves His lost creation and extends grace to us, empowering believers to love Him and others at a higher standard than the law.
Romans 5:7–8; 2 Corinthians 5:14–18; Romans 6:11–14; Matthew 5:21–28; Romans 8:2–4; Acts 9:1–22, 26:1–23

Deeply experiencing grace teaches us about righteousness, which empowers us to overcome sin and failure. The Father's love keeps us from focusing on sin or hiding in shame if we fail.
Ephesians 3:14–21; 2 Corinthians 3:17–18; Titus 2:11–13; Colossians 3:1–5; Acts 2:14–41

God's grace breaks the mentality that says "I am a powerless victim of circumstances" and creates a new identity that declares, "In Christ, I am a victorious overcomer, no matter the situation."
John 16:33; 1 John 4:4; Romans 8:31–32, 35–39; 1 Corinthians 15:57; 2 Corinthians 2:14; Deuteronomy 28:13; Jeremiah 29:11

WHAT DOES THIS MEAN?

Our old self is dead—crucified with Christ. We are free and empowered to live in His righteousness and share in His sufferings.
Romans 6:1–7, 8:1–9; Galatians 2:19–21; 2 Corinthians 3:4–6; Philippians 3:8–11

R

God is always loving and is passionate about fulfilling His purposes for our lives.
John 3:16; Romans 5:8; Philippians 2:13; Ephesians 1:4; Romans 8:38–39; 2 Peter 3:9; 2 Timothy 2:13; Romans 11:29

God has given us joy that is greater than any circumstances we face.
Isaiah 54:1; Nehemiah 8:10; Hebrews 12:2; James 1:2–3; Psalm 27:6

We grow into Christ-like, spiritual maturity when we allow His love and power to transform us.
2 Corinthians 3:17–18; Ephesians 3:14–21; 2 Corinthians 12:9; 1 Corinthians 3:1–3; Romans 12:2; Philippians 3:12; 2 Timothy 1:9; Ephesians 1:4, 5:1–2

We partner with the Holy Spirit and fellow believers to be changed and led into personal transformation.
James 5:13–16; Matthew 18:15–20; Philippians 2:13; 1 Corinthians 15:10; Ephesians 2:8–9; Romans 12:2; Galatians 6:1–2, 5:16; Titus 2:11–13

God has given us access to unlimited resources so that we can do His good works and change the world.
Matthew 18:18, 28:18–20; John 14:12–15; Ephesians 2:4–10; 1 John 4:17

God's grace empowers us to be unique, to dream, and to create with Him.
1 Peter 4:10; 1 Corinthians 12:7; John 15:7, 16, 16:24; Ephesians 3:10–11; Romans 8:18–19

DO NOT MISUNDERSTAND

None of us has attained perfection; there is still room for us all to grow.
Philippians 3:12–15; 1 Corinthians 13:12; 1 John 1:8; James 3:2; 2 Corinthians 3:18; Ephesians 4:13–15

We may still be tempted by old sinful habits, but we recognize that these temptations have nothing to do with our identities.
1 Corinthians 6:9–11; Galatians 5:24; 1 Corinthians 10:13; Romans 6:12–13; James 1:13–15

We are never content with sin remaining in our lives.
Ephesians 5:1–4; Galatians 5:13; Romans 6:1–2; 1 Thessalonians 4:3–5; 1 John 1:8–10; Romans 12:1–3

We co-labor with Jesus so that He gets His full reward.
Matthew 28:19; Mark 16:15, 20; Ephesians 2:10; Philippians 2:13, 3:13–14; 1 Corinthians 3:9; 2 Corinthians 6:1

We choose daily to live in the fullness of His abundant grace.
Lamentations 3:22–23; Luke 9:23; Galatians 5:1; Hebrews 12:1–3

There is a hell and not everyone will choose salvation.
2 Corinthians 5:10; Matthew 10:28; Hebrews 9:27; Matthew 25:31–46

Our desires need to be submitted to the will of God.
Proverbs 3:5–6, 16:9; James 4:13–15; Philippians 2:13; Romans 6:12–13

Our physical bodies are a blessing, declared good by God in the beginning and restored to holiness through Christ.
Genesis 1:27, 31; Romans 8:11, 6:12–13; 1 Corinthians 6:19–20

We have a responsibility to steward and manage the grace, resources, and gifts we have been given.
1 Peter 4:10; Colossians 3:23–24; Matthew 25:14–30; Romans 6:13; Genesis 1:28, 2:15

Write one or two of your own "What Does This Mean?" statements for *Responsive to Grace*, along with one or two supporting Scriptures.

-

-

Try to think of one or two other ways the core value *Responsive to Grace* could potentially be misunderstood, along with one or two Scriptures to correct these misunderstandings.

-

-

R

WHAT IS GOD SAYING TO ME?

As you read each of the four core value definitions and supporting scriptures below, take time to wait quietly with the Lord, asking Him, *"What are You saying to me about this core value?"* Use the space below each definition to journal what comes to your mind and spirit as you listen: thoughts, impressions, Scriptures, pictures, etc...

We joyfully experience the astounding, undeserved love of God and His ongoing power to transform us. His transforming love and power are inseparable from one another.
Ephesians 2:8–10; Romans 5:6–11; Mark 5:1–20

"For God so loved the world, that He gave His only begotten Son, that whoever believes in Him shall not perish, but have eternal life. For God did not send the Son into the world to judge the world, but that the world might be saved through Him." - John 3:16–17

"Just as He chose us in Him before the foundation of the world, that we would be holy and blameless before Him. In love He predestined us to adoption as sons through Jesus Christ to Himself, according to the kind intention of His will." - Ephesians 1:4–5

God scandalously loves His lost creation and extends grace to us, empowering believers to love Him and others at a higher standard than the law.
2 Corinthians 5:14–18; Romans 6:11–14; Matthew 5:21–28; Romans 8:2–4; Acts 9:1–22, 26:1–23

"For one will hardly die for a righteous man; though perhaps for the good man someone would dare even to die. But God demonstrates His own love toward us, in that while we were yet sinners, Christ died for us." - Romans 5:7–8

Deeply experiencing grace teaches us about righteousness, which empowers us to overcome sin and failure. The Father's love keeps us from focusing on sin or hiding in shame if we fail.
2 Corinthians 3:17–18; Titus 2:11–13; Colossians 3:1–5; Acts 2:14–41

"For this reason I bow my knees before the Father, from whom every family in heaven and on earth derives its name, that He would grant you, according to the riches of His glory, to be strengthened with power through His Spirit in the inner man, so that Christ may dwell in your hearts through faith; and that you, being rooted and grounded in love, may be able to comprehend with all the saints what is the breadth and length and height and depth, and to know the love of Christ which surpasses knowledge, that you may be filled up to all the fullness of God. Now to Him who is able to do far more abundantly beyond all that we ask or think, according to the power that works within us, to Him be the glory in the church and in Christ Jesus to all generations forever and ever. Amen." - Ephesians 3:14–21

R

God's grace breaks the mentality that says "I am a powerless victim of circumstances" and creates a new identity that declares, "In Christ, I am a victorious overcomer, no matter the situation."
Romans 8:31–32, 35–39; 1 Corinthians 15:57; 2 Corinthians 2:14; Deuteronomy 28:13; Jeremiah 29:11

"These things I have spoken to you, so that in Me you may have peace. In the world you have tribulation, but take courage; I have overcome the world." - John 16:33

"You are from God, little children, and have overcome them; because greater is He who is in you than he who is in the world." - 1 John 4:4

ACTIVATIONS

Spend 10 or 15 minutes reflecting on how well you are living in the fullness of God's love and grace. Ask the Holy Spirit the following questions, being careful to wait quietly for a few moments in between each question to give Him the opportunity to speak to your spirit. Journal anything He may show you.

- Are there any areas in my life where I have been living out of a mindset of punishment or condemnation? If so, what are they?

- Do I emotionally or spiritually beat myself up when I think I failed or didn't do something right?

- Do I ever have negative thoughts about myself? Do I ever have feelings of self-hatred? If so, in what situations or circumstances do those thoughts or feelings come up?

- Do I have a tendency to live in isolation? If so, is there something I'm afraid of?

- Do I find it difficult to receive love from God and/or people? If so, why?

Share your answers with a trusted friend or family member. Ask him or her to pray with you concerning any areas the Lord showed you, such as the lie that punishing or condemning yourself enough will make you more perfect, more loveable, or more Christ-like. As you close your prayer time, wait quietly for three or four minutes to give the Holy Spirit time to renew your heart and mind with truth. Invite Him to invade every area of your spirit, mind, and body with His love and expect Him to do it!

TESTIMONIES

"For years, it controlled me. I felt dirty, ashamed and incapable of pursuing what I wanted in life. I'd been crying out for years but nothing ever changed. I was addicted to online porn and I was desperate for God to come through for me. Many people would tell me, 'You just need to give it to God.' But that didn't click for me. I was desperate for acceptance and identity and I didn't believe God could fill that void in my life. One day, I experienced God as my Father. His love washed over me and in that moment my heart and eyes were opened to truth and freedom. The scale had tipped. My heart's desire began to turn towards the love of my Father rather than the urge to fill my need for love and acceptance with pornography. After I encountered God as my loving Father, I woke up one morning and discovered I no longer had the urge to view pornography. God had delivered me from my addiction to porn! I now live with joy instead of shame, confidence instead of insecurity. I have new trust in God's power to help me live a pure and free life. My freedom from porn was the beginning of total transformation in every area. My whole life I relied on compulsive eating to get me through each day. That addiction is also gone! When I realized the Holy Spirit can comfort me in a way food never can, losing weight became easy. In less than nine months, I lost eighty pounds!"

-JOSH T.

Write a story about what happened when you or someone you know responded to the undeserved love and transforming power of God's grace.

MY MESSAGE

Whether preaching or talking with your family at the dinner table, use this sermon preparation guide to organize your thoughts so you can help others understand what it means to be responsive to God's grace.

My favorite scriptures for this core value:

My interpretation of these scriptures:

The key points I want to communicate:

The key phrase from the testimony I'll share as an example of this core value:

Give an example of how these truths could be applied to a real-life situation:

What change, inspiration, impartation, and/or call to action do I want others to embrace after learning how to respond to God's grace?

HOW AM I DOING?

Take a few minutes to reread the core value definitions at the beginning of this chapter and then rate yourself from 1-5 in each area below to help you identify strengths and opportunities for growth. Use this information to help you create personal growth goals on the following page.

1 / NEVER **2** / RARELY **3** / SOMETIMES **4** / OFTEN **5** / ALWAYS

R

I KNOW I AM RESPONSIVE TO GRACE

____ I can articulate it.

____ I have experienced it in personal and/or corporate settings.

____ I have a growing affection for it and I desire to apply it.

I DO THIS CORE VALUE

____ I am taking risks and sharing testimonies as I practice this core value.

____ I invite people into my life who exhibit, call out, and give me feedback in this value.

I BELIEVE THIS CORE VALUE

____ I have identified and replaced opposing beliefs and behaviors that hinder my growth in this area.

____ My level of hope and expectation has increased in this area.

____ I usually view and respond to life through the lens of it.

I REPRODUCE RESPONSIVE TO GRACE

____ I bring the strength of it as I serve others and build community.

____ I am intentional in reproducing it in others and can see their progress.

____ I have stories of how others have recognized and been impacted by it in my life.

I AM RESPONSIVE TO GRACE

____ I have consistently lived each of the prior stages for many years in a variety of settings.

____ It is my natural response as I make decisions and respond to situations in my everyday life.

____ I am an innovator, explorer and articulator of it and people seek my wisdom concerning it.

GROWING IN THIS CORE VALUE

Using your personal assessment from the previous page, ask Holy Spirit to help you write a short-term and long-term goal for each of the following areas. Remember to make your goals time-specific, measurable, and realistic. Choose one to focus on this week and, as you accomplish it, come back and check it off so you can see your growth. Below are some examples to get you started.

MYSELF

- ☐ Today I will set an alert on my phone/computer to remind myself twice a day that my old self was crucified with Christ and I am now empowered to live victoriously in His righteousness.
- ☐ Short-range goal: ______
- ☐ Long-range goal: ______

MY HOME/FAMILY

- ☐ For the next 48 hours, I'll focus on becoming free from the lie that I am a powerless victim of circumstances or other people's choices and, instead, become focused on my new identity that declares, "I am a victorious overcomer, no matter the situation!"
- ☐ Short-range goal: ______
- ☐ Long-range goal: ______

MY PLACE OF WORK/SCHOOL

- ☐ On Tuesday and Thursday this week I will ask the Lord to give me one opportunity to practically demonstrate His extravagant love and grace to one of my coworkers/classmates.
- ☐ Short-range goal: ______
- ☐ Long-range goal: ______

OTHER

- ☐ ______

NOTES

R

R

I DO NOT

PURSUE GOD

TO GET MORE;

I PURSUE GOD

BECAUSE I KNOW

THERE IS MORE.

ERIC JOHNSON

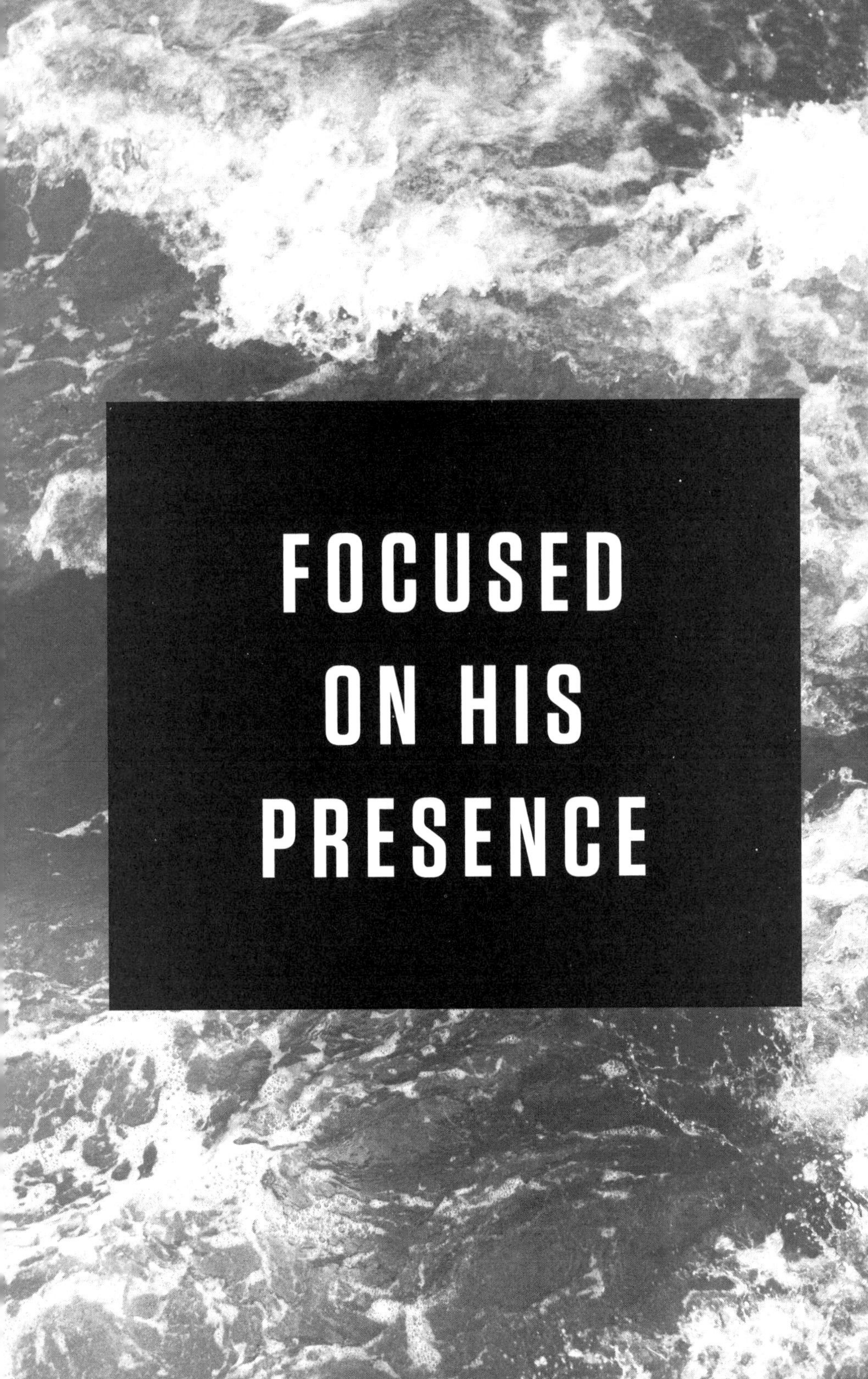
FOCUSED
ON HIS
PRESENCE

FOCUSED ON HIS PRESENCE

DEFINING THE CORE VALUE

Our first ministry is to God. As we behold Him, we are moved to worship with joyous passion.
Psalm 27:4; Luke 10:39–42; James 4:8; Psalm 1:1–3, 23:6, 26:8; John 4:23; Psalm 22:3

God delights in us and He has always desired to be with us. We focus on His presence because we have discovered that He is focused on us.
Ephesians 1:4–5; Zephaniah 3:17; Jeremiah 31:3; Psalm 65:4; 1 John 3:1; Revelation 3:20; 1 John 4:19

Purposefully cultivating a hunger for God's manifest presence and an openness to experiencing the Holy Spirit deepens our friendship with God and our awareness that we carry His presence for the sake of the world.
Psalm 73:28, 107:9; John 1:16; Matthew 5:6; Isaiah 55:1–2; 1 Corinthians 3:16

As a lifestyle, we practice recognizing God's presence while we minister to others, attempting to say what He is saying and do what He is doing.
John 5:19–20, 30, 12:49–50, 14:10; 1 John 4:16–17

WHAT DOES THIS MEAN?

We worship and have fellowship with God throughout the day in all aspects of life, such as prayer, the Word, creativity, music, nature, family, work, and friendships.
1 John 1:3; Matthew 6:6–15; 1 Corinthians 1:9; 1 Thessalonians 5:16–18; Psalm 104; Colossians 3:16-17

God has made us a dwelling place for His Spirit.
1 Corinthians 6:19–20; 2 Timothy 1:14; Colossians 2:9–10

As we draw near to God, He draws near to us.
James 4:8; Matthew 5:6, 6:33

The Holy Spirit's presence motivates us toward love and toward changing the world.
Matthew 28:18–20; Joel 2:28; Acts 1:8; Romans 5:5

We are called to behold God face to face, allowing nothing to come between Him and us. As we do this, we are transformed into the image of Christ.
Exodus 20:3; 2 Corinthians 3:16–18, 5:18–20; Matthew 22:37

Connected to God, we are filled with joy and peace and are empowered to take risks to extend the Kingdom.
Psalm 13:5; Hebrews 1:9; John 15; Acts 1:8; Romans 14:17, 15:13

Every part of a Christian's life is sacred and meant to be holy. We do not live with the false mindset that life is divided into the "sacred" or the "secular." Rather, God values and is involved in every area of our lives. The Holy Spirit lives in us, so everything we do and everywhere we go is sacred.
Colossians 1:16–20, 3:23; 1 Timothy 4:3–5; Revelation 11:15; 1 Corinthians 10:31

DO NOT MISUNDERSTAND

Being focused on His presence doesn't mean Christians should spend all their time in private worship, disconnected from the rest of life.
Hebrews 10:25; 1 Corinthians 4:12; Galatians 6:10; Matthew 18:20; John 17:15, 18

Not everything supernatural is from God; we must use our discernment.
1 John 4:1; Acts 13:6–12, 16:16–18; Philippians 1:9–10; Hebrews 5:14

Physical manifestations of the Holy Spirit are not an indicator of our spiritual maturity.
1 Corinthians 13:1–3, 13; Matthew 7:21–23

God's presence is just as much at work in the secular world as it is inside the church.
Psalm 139:7–12; Matthew 5:44–45; Habakkuk 2:14; Numbers 14:21; Romans 5:20

The Holy Spirit leads us into a Presence-focused lifestyle, not a self-focused lifestyle.
Matthew 16:24–25; Luke 14:27; 1 Peter 2:21; Hebrews 12:1–2

Write one or two of your own "What Does This Mean?" statements for *Focused on His Presence,* along with one or two supporting Scriptures.

-
-

Try to think of one or two other ways the core value *Focused on His Presence* could potentially be misunderstood, along with one or two Scriptures to correct these misunderstandings.

-
-

F

WHAT IS GOD SAYING TO ME?

As you read each of the four core value definitions and supporting scriptures below, take time to wait quietly with the Lord, asking Him, *"What are You saying to me about this core value?"* Use the space below each definition to journal what comes to your mind and spirit as you listen: thoughts, impressions, Scriptures, pictures, etc...

Our first ministry is to God. As we behold Him, we are moved to worship with joyous passion.
Luke 10:39–42; Psalm 1:1–3, 23:6, 26:8; John 4:23; Psalm 22:3

"One thing I have asked from the Lord, that I shall seek: That I may dwell in the house of the Lord all the days of my life, to behold the beauty of the Lord and to meditate in His temple."
- Psalm 27:4

"Draw near to God and He will draw near to you. Cleanse your hands, you sinners; and purify your hearts, you double-minded." - James 4:8

God delights in us and He has always desired to be with us. We focus on His presence because we have discovered that He is focused on us.
Jeremiah 31:3; Psalm 65:4; 1 John 3:1; Revelation 3:20; 1 John 4:19

"Just as He chose us in Him before the foundation of the world, that we would be holy and blameless before Him. In love He predestined us to adoption as sons through Jesus Christ to Himself, according to the kind intention of His will." - Ephesians 1:4–5

"The Lord your God is in your midst, a victorious warrior. He will exult over you with joy, He will be quiet in His love, He will rejoice over you with shouts of joy." - Zephaniah 3:17

Purposely cultivating a hunger for God's manifest presence and an openness to experiencing the Holy Spirit deepens our friendship with God and our awareness that we carry His presence for the sake of the world.
John 1:16; Matthew 5:6; Isaiah 55:1–2; 1 Corinthians 3:16

"But as for me, the nearness of God is my good; I have made the Lord God my refuge, that I may tell of all Your works." - Psalm 73:28

"For He has satisfied the thirsty soul, and the hungry soul He has filled with what is good."
- Psalm 107:9

As a lifestyle, we practice recognizing God's presence while we minister to others, attempting to say what He is saying and do what He is doing.
John 12:49–50, 14:10; 1 John 4:16–17

"Therefore Jesus answered and was saying to them, 'Truly, truly, I say to you, the Son can do nothing of Himself, unless it is something He sees the Father doing; for whatever the Father does, these things the Son also does in like manner. For the Father loves the Son, and shows Him all things that He Himself is doing; and the Father will show Him greater works than these, so that you will marvel.'" - John 5:19–20

"I can do nothing on My own initiative. As I hear, I judge; and My judgment is just, because I do not seek My own will, but the will of Him who sent Me." - John 5:30

ACTIVATIONS

At the beginning of the week, set reminders somewhere you're sure to see them, like your bathroom mirror or computer, to help you focus on His presence throughout your day. For example, put a sign on your mirror to remind yourself to pray, "Baptize me afresh in Your Spirit!" every morning and every evening. Or, right before you start work or school, set a reminder on your computer that says, "My hands are anointed to heal the sick right now!" At the end of the week, remove these reminders and reflect on how this impacted your life. Maybe you'll decide you want to put up new reminders for next week.

Ask God for one or two prophetic signs to help you refocus on Him throughout your day and then ask Him what He wants you to do when you see those signs. For example, every time you see the color yellow let that be a reminder that your life is going from glory to glory. Double or triple numbers could be a reminder to take a moment and pause what you are doing to turn your heart and mind to the Lord in love and adoration.

- My prophetic sign to remind me to focus on His presence:

- What God wants me to do when I see this sign:

- My prophetic sign to remind me to focus on His presence:

- What God wants me to do when I see this sign:

TESTIMONIES

"As soon as I saw the guy giving out free sausage samples, the thought entered my mind, 'He has a messed up knee from a sports injury in high school.' I work at a Christian t-shirt kiosk in our local mall. Often, when customers come to my booth, God tells me where they have pain in their bodies. I ask if I can pray for them and many times they get healed. I was having a lot of success so I started taking more risks and getting creative in how I prayed for healing. The day I saw the guy giving out sausage samples in front of Hickory Farms, I decided to take a risk. I told him the thought I had about his knee and he said, 'Yes, I have an injury in both my knees from high school football.' I asked if I could pray for him, but he said no because he was working. Determined to see him experience the love and power of God, I didn't give up. Instead, I asked for one of the toothpicks he was using and I prayed over it. He held it for a few seconds and I asked him what he felt. He said, 'My knees feel really warm all of a sudden.' Then he bent his knees and realized they were completely healed. I see him at work all the time now and ever since I gave him that toothpick there's been no pain in his knees!"

-DAVID W.

Write one or two stories of something that happened in your life or someone you know as a result of being focused on His presence.

-

-

F

MY MESSAGE

Whether preaching on the streets of Kathmandu or talking with friends at church, use this sermon preparation guide to organize your thoughts so you can help others understand what it means to be focused on His presence.

My favorite scriptures for this core value:

My interpretation of these scriptures:

The key points I want to communicate:

The key phrase from the testimony I'll share as an example of this core value:

Give an example of how these truths could be applied to a real-life situation:

What change, inspiration, impartation, and/or call to action do I want others to embrace after learning about being focused on His presence?

HOW AM I DOING?

Take a few minutes to reread the core value definitions at the beginning of this chapter and then rate yourself from 1–5 in each area below to help you identify strengths and opportunities for growth. Use this information to help you create personal growth goals on the following page.

1 / NEVER **2** / RARELY **3** / SOMETIMES **4** / OFTEN **5** / ALWAYS

F

I KNOW THIS CORE VALUE

____ I can articulate it.

____ I have experienced it in personal and/or corporate settings.

____ I have a growing affection for it and I desire to apply it.

I AM FOCUSED ON HIS PRESENCE

____ I am taking risks and sharing testimonies as I practice this core value.

____ I invite people into my life who exhibit, call out, and give me feedback in this value.

I BELIEVE THIS CORE VALUE

____ I have identified and replaced opposing beliefs and behaviors that hinder my growth in this area.

____ My level of hope and expectation has increased in this area.

____ I usually view and respond to life through the lens of it.

I REPRODUCE BEING FOCUSED ON HIS PRESENCE

____ I have it as a priority in my life.

____ I am intentional in reproducing it in others and can see their progress.

____ I have stories of how others have recognized and been impacted by it in my life.

I AM THIS CORE VALUE

____ I have consistently lived each of the prior stages for many years in a variety of settings.

____ I am an innovator, explorer, and articulator of it and people seek my wisdom concerning it.

____ I understand the spiritual authority I have in this area and intentionally influence those around me.

GROWING IN THIS CORE VALUE

Using your personal assessment from the previous page, ask Holy Spirit to help you write a short-term and long-term goal for each of the following areas. Remember to make your goals time-specific, measurable, and realistic. Choose one to focus on this week and, as you accomplish it, come back and check it off so you can see your growth. Below are some examples to get you started.

MYSELF

- ☐ For the next four days, I will purposely cultivate a hunger for God's manifest presence by spending 30 minutes in worship each day.
- ☐ Short-range goal: ______
- ☐ Long-range goal: ______

MY HOME/FAMILY

- ☐ Today I will practice recognizing God's presence while I talk with my family by focusing on saying what He's saying and doing what He's doing.
- ☐ Short-range goal: ______
- ☐ Long-range goal: ______

MY PLACE OF WORK/SCHOOL

- ☐ This week I will set aside a few moments throughout my day to worship God at work and/or school.
- ☐ Short-range goal: ______
- ☐ Long-range goal: ______

OTHER

- ☐ ______
- ☐ ______

NOTES

F

F

THE EXPERIENCE OF INTIMACY—OF BEING COMPLETELY KNOWN AND ACCEPTED, AND COMPLETELY KNOWING AND ACCEPTING IN RETURN—IS THE MOST SATISFYING EXPERIENCE WE CAN HAVE AS HUMANS.

DANNY SILK

CREATING
HEALTHY
FAMILY

CREATING HEALTHY FAMILY

DEFINING THE CORE VALUE

We are adopted into God's family, so we intentionally create family and community wherever we go.
Ephesians 1:5, 2:19; Matthew 12:48–50; Galatians 6:10; Romans 8:15–16; 1 Peter 2:17; Acts 2:41–47

We think like healthy family members and do what's best for the whole environment, mutually submitting to one another in love and not being selfish.
Philippians 2:3; Romans 12:9–21; Ephesians 5:21; Galatians 5:13; 1 Corinthians 13; Ruth 1:16–17

In covenant relationships, we purposely grow our capacity to trust and be trusted as we empower and confront one another in order to live out who we truly are.
Matthew 18:15; Luke 17:3–4; Ephesians 4:15–16; 1 Corinthians 4:14–21; 1 Thessalonians 5:14; 1 Samuel 20

We are loyal, which is demonstrated most radically when people fail. We do not punish and abandon those who fail in order to save face or show we hate sin, but instead we commit to helping them be restored.
Galatians 6:1; Matthew 18:15; John 8:1–11; Psalm 141:5; John 21

WHAT DOES THIS MEAN?

God the Father, Jesus, and the Holy Spirit have brought us into their intimacy and family. From their love and wisdom, we build healthy families and communities.
John 17:23, 15:15–16; 1 John 1:3–4; Ephesians 3:14–21; 1 John 3:1; Hebrews 10:24–25

Jesus explicitly created us to live in community; people are most alive when planted in a healthy family of believers.
Genesis 2:18, 1:26–28; Acts 4:23–35; 1 Corinthians 12:21–27; Psalm 133:1; Ephesians 3:14–20

The way we love people is a direct reflection of our love for God.
John 13:35; 1 John 4:20; Proverbs 14:31; Matthew 10:42, 25:34–40; Hebrews 6:10

C

Love for ourselves, which springs from God's great love for us, is vital in truly caring for others and creating healthy families.
Matthew 22:37–39; Romans 12:3; Ephesians 5:1–2, 28–30

We draw from the Holy Spirit's gifts and graces in the whole family of God, not just from those in leadership.
Romans 12:4–10; 1 Peter 4:10–11; 1 Corinthians 12; Matthew 10:41

We value and honor each other, even when we disagree.
Philippians 2:3–16; Romans 12:4, 10; 1 Peter 2:13–17, 5:5–6

We do nothing out of selfish ambition or gain. Instead, we intentionally partner with others to seek mutual benefit in everything we do.
Philippians 2:1–4; Romans 12:10; Ephesians 5:21; James 4:1–12; Hebrews 10:24–26

We are responsible to speak up with loving confrontation when others in the family of God sin, based on the truth that, as a new creation in Christ, they are too amazing to be behaving that way.
Matthew 18:15–17; Galatians 6:1–2; Luke 9:54–56; 2 Corinthians 3:16–18, 5:17, 7:9–10; Ephesians 2:10; Philippians 2:13; Psalm 139:14

WHAT DOES THIS MEAN? (CONTINUED)

Forgiveness is our standard; everyone is given the opportunity to rebuild trust in the community.
Ephesians 4:32; Matthew 18:21–35; Luke 17:3–4, 23:34; James 5:16-20

We believe in God's design and instruction that loving, life-long marriage between a man and a woman is the healthiest and, ultimately, the only structure upon which to build a stable, thriving society.
Hebrews 13:4; Genesis 1:27–28; Matthew 5:32; 1 Corinthians 6:9–11, 18; 1 Thessalonians 4:3–5; Mark 10:1–12

DO NOT MISUNDERSTAND

Not all Christian communities are demonstrating healthy relationships.
1 Corinthians 3:1–3; Galatians 6:1–2; 1 Corinthians 4:14–15, 5:6

People who have experienced broken marriages and/or families are not disqualified from greatness, as Jesus is more than able to forgive and restore them into healthy, holy families and communities.
1 John 1:9; Romans 8:1–3; John 4:1–42; 1 Corinthians 6:9–11; 2 Corinthians 5:16–17

We recognize that it is possible for someone to behave their way out of the community, so sometimes it is unwise and unsafe for a community to extend grace at the same level that God does.
Ephesians 5:11; Romans 16:17–19; Titus 3:9–11; 2 Timothy 3:1–6; Matthew 18:17; 1 Corinthians 5:4–6; 1 Timothy 1:18–20

Write two of your own "What Does This Mean?" statements for *Creating Healthy Family*, along with one or two supporting Scriptures.

-

-

Try to think of one or two other ways the core value *Creating Healthy Family* could potentially be misunderstood, along with one or two Scriptures to correct these misunderstandings.

-

-

C

WHAT IS GOD SAYING TO ME?

As you read each of the four core value definitions and supporting scriptures below, take time to wait quietly with the Lord, asking Him, *"What are You saying to me about this core value?"* Use the space below each definition to journal what comes to your mind and spirit as you listen: thoughts, impressions, Scriptures, pictures, etc...

We are adopted into God's family, so we intentionally create family and community wherever we go.
Matthew 12:48–50; Galatians 6:10; Romans 8:15–16; 1 Peter 2:17; Acts 2:41–47

"He predestined us to adoption as sons through Jesus Christ to Himself, according to the kind intention of His will." - Ephesians 1:5

"Now, therefore, you are no longer strangers and foreigners, but fellow citizens with the saints and members of the household of God." - Ephesians 2:19

We think like healthy family members and do what's best for the whole environment, mutually submitting to one another in love and not being selfish.
Romans 12:9–21; Galatians 5:13; 1 Corinthians 13; Ruth 1:16–17

"Let nothing be done through selfish ambition or conceit, but in lowliness of mind let each esteem others better than himself." - Philippians 2:3

"Submitting to one another in the fear of God." - Ephesians 5:21

In covenant relationships, we purposely grow our capacity to trust and be trusted as we empower and confront one another in order to live out who we truly are.
Ephesians 4:15–16; 1 Corinthians 4:14–21; 1 Thessalonians 5:14; 1 Samuel 20

"Moreover if your brother sins against you, go and tell him his fault between you and him alone. If he hears you, you have gained your brother." - Matthew 18:15

"Be on your guard! If your brother sins, rebuke him; and if he repents, forgive him. And if he sins against you seven times a day, and returns to you seven times, saying, 'I repent,' forgive him." - Luke 17:3–4

We are loyal, which is demonstrated most radically when people fail. We do not punish and abandon those who fail in order to save face or show we hate sin, but instead we commit to helping them be restored.
John 8:1–11; Psalm 141:5; John 21

"Brethren, if a man is overtaken in any trespass, you who are spiritual restore such a one in a spirit of gentleness, considering yourself lest you also be tempted." - Galatians 6:1

"Moreover if your brother sins against you, go and tell him his fault between you and him alone. If he hears you, you have gained your brother." - Matthew 18:15

C

ACTIVATIONS

Ask two of your closest family members or friends how they feel your relationship with them is going. Ask if there is anything you could change or do differently to help your relationship become stronger and more intimate. Write down whatever feedback they give you and ask the Lord to show you what changes you could make in response.

Take five minutes and call, write a text, or send an email to your family members or closest friends and tell them what you love about them and why you are grateful to have them in your life.

Ask the Lord to show you if there are any areas in your life where you have not been vulnerable or fully honest with the people closest to you and arrange a time to share openly with them. Or, if you have a secret you haven't shared with anyone, make yourself vulnerable and bring your secret into the light with a trusted family member or friend.

TESTIMONIES

"Surprised to see my brother calling so early in the morning, I picked up. 'Hey, man! What's up?' I'd been praying for my whole family for three years and believed God would touch them powerfully but never expected to hear what he was about to tell me. He had just personally experienced God's love and power as he watched one of the testimony videos I posted on Facebook showing people getting healed and transformed by God. I could hear the tears in his voice as he recounted it all to me. He had been into drugs for many years and had never been able to think clearly until that day! 'God transformed my life when I watched that video,' he said of the experience. 'I instantly felt clarity and peace of mind and got completely free from drugs!' For the first time in our lives he opened up to me. He said he felt so loved by God and excited for this new chapter in his life and asked me to help him become a better father and husband. I couldn't stop smiling when he said, 'I have always known you to be the real deal but now I want to be the real deal!'"

-ANDREY K.

Write one or two testimonies about a time when you or someone you know was impacted by healthy family.

-

-

MY MESSAGE

Whether leading an outback wilderness experience or sitting around with family after a holiday dinner, use this sermon preparation guide to organize your thoughts so you can help others understand the value of creating healthy family and community.

My favorite scriptures for this core value:

My interpretation of these scriptures:

Key points I want to communicate:

The key phrase from the testimony I'll share as an example of this core value:

Example of how these truths could be applied to a real-life situation:

The change, inspiration, impartation, and/or call to action I want others to embrace after learning about creating healthy family:

HOW AM I DOING?

Take a few minutes to reread the core value definitions at the beginning of this chapter and then rate yourself from 1–5 in each area below to help you identify strengths and opportunities for growth. Use this information to help you create personal growth goals on the following page.

1 / NEVER **2** / RARELY **3** / SOMETIMES **4** / OFTEN **5** / ALWAYS

I KNOW THIS CORE VALUE

____ I can articulate it.

____ I have experienced it in personal and/or corporate settings.

____ I have a growing affection for it and I desire to apply it.

I CREATE HEALTHY FAMILY

____ I am taking risks and sharing testimonies as I practice this core value.

____ I invite people into my life who exhibit, call out, and give me feedback in this value.

I BELIEVE IN CREATING HEALTHY FAMILY

____ I have identified and replaced opposing beliefs and behaviors that hinder my growth in this area.

____ My level of hope and expectation has increased in this area.

____ I usually view and respond to life through the lens of it.

I REPRODUCE THIS CORE VALUE

____ I have it as a priority in my life.

____ I bring the strength of it as I serve others and build community.

____ I am intentionally reproducing it in others and can see their progress.

I AM THIS CORE VALUE

____ I have consistently lived each of the prior stages for many years in a variety of settings.

____ It is my natural response as I make decisions and respond to situations in my everyday life.

____ I understand the spiritual authority I have in this area and intentionally influence those around me.

C

GROWING IN THIS CORE VALUE

Using your personal assessment from the previous page, ask Holy Spirit to help you write a short-term and long-term goal for each of the following areas. Remember to make your goals time-specific, measurable, and realistic. Choose one to focus on this week and, as you accomplish it, come back and check it off so you can see your growth. Below are some examples to get you started.

MYSELF

- ☐ Before the end of the week, I will take time to meditate on *Creating Healthy Family* and ask the Holy Spirit to help me identify and replace any lies I've been believing or behaviors that have been hindering my growth in this area.
- ☐ Short-range goal:
- ☐ Long-range goal:

MY HOME/FAMILY

- ☐ I will do something special and unexpected for one of my housemates/family members in the next 48 hours to show them my appreciation for them.
- ☐ Short-range goal:
- ☐ Long-range goal:

MY PLACE OF WORK/SCHOOL

- ☐ This month I will organize a social gathering at my workplace or school to intentionally create family and community.
- ☐ Short-range goal:
- ☐ Long-range goal:

OTHER

- ☐
- ☐

NOTES

C

C

YOU GET FAITH BY
STUDYING THE WORD.
STUDY THAT WORD UNTIL
SOMETHING IN YOU
"KNOWS THAT YOU KNOW"
AND THAT YOU DO NOT JUST
HOPE THAT YOU KNOW.

CARRIE JUDD MONTGOMERY

GOD'S WORD TRANSFORMS

GOD'S WORD TRANSFORMS

DEFINING THE CORE VALUE

The goal of Scripture is to bring us into a relationship with the Author and transform us into His likeness.
John 5:39–40; 2 Timothy 3:15–17; Matthew 4:4; 2 Corinthians 3:15–18; James 1:22–25; Ephesians 5:25–27; Psalm 119:11; Luke 24:13–35

As God encounters us in His Word, faith is released into our lives. Studying God's truth empowers us to believe in who He is, who we are, and how He wants us to live.
Romans 10:17; 1 Thessalonians 2:13; John 17:17; Matthew 7:24–28; Colossians 3:15–17; John 8:31–32; Psalm 119:105; Romans 15:4; 1 Corinthians 10:1–13; Acts 8:26–40

The primary lens through which we interpret the Bible is the person, life, and redemptive work of Jesus, because He is the most complete revelation of who God is and what God cares about.
John 5:37–47; Luke 24:25–32; John 1:14, 14:9–11; Colossians 1:15–20, 2:9; Hebrews 1:1–3; 2 Peter 1:16–21

The Bible is the source of infallible truth and authority by which we judge all insight and prophetic revelation.
2 Timothy 3:15–17; Matthew 22:29; John 8:31–32; 2 Thessalonians 2:13–15; 2 Peter 1:16–21; Proverbs 30:5–6; Psalm 119:160; Matthew 4:1–11

WHAT DOES THIS MEAN?

The Bible should lead us into an ever-growing relationship with the Father, Son, and Holy Spirit.
John 5:39–40; 2 Timothy 3:15–17; Psalm 119:11; John 1:14, 14:6

The Bible is infallible, but our interpretation of it might not be.
John 5:39–40; 2 Timothy 2:14–18; Luke 24:25–32

Through relationship with the Holy Spirit and a Spirit-filled community, we seek to accurately interpret and apply the Bible, which helps to guard against deception and misapplication.
John 16:12–15; 2 Corinthians 3:4–6; 1 Corinthians 2:9–11, 16; 1 John 4:1; Matthew 7:15; Hebrews 4:12

We come alive and are transformed as we study, hear and act upon God's words spoken to us in a particular moment.
Romans 10:17; 2 Timothy 2:14–16; Matthew 4:4; Hebrews 4:2; John 6:63; Isaiah 55:11

G

As we are in Christ, we participate in the fulfilment of the promises that God gave us in Scripture.
2 Peter 1:3–8; 2 Corinthians 1:20; Numbers 23:19; 1 Thessalonians 5:24

When we declare God's words, we partner with Him in transforming the world.
Proverbs 18:21; Joel 3:10; Isaiah 54:1; Acts 3:6–7; Jonah 3:3–10; Matthew 4:1–11

We need to keep listening and keep asking God questions because He can reveal more and more truth over time.
John 16:12–13; Genesis 22; James 1:5; Matthew 7:7–11; Genesis 18:16–33

DO NOT MISUNDERSTAND

God is never boxed in by our current understanding of His Word.
John 8:1–11; Matthew 12:1–13; Matthew 22:29; Job 42:2–5; Act 11:1–18

Studying the Word and experiencing God's presence should never be separated from one another.
John 5:39–40; 2 Timothy 2:14–19; Acts 11:1–18

It is possible for a Christian to be deceived.
Galatians 3:1; 1 John 4:1; Ephesians 4:22–27; 1 Peter 5:8; Colossians 2:6–8

We should always judge and evaluate an interpretation of Scripture.
Acts 17:11; 1 John 4:1; Matthew 7:15–20; 2 Peter 2:1–3

The devil can use Scripture in an attempt to deceive a Christian.
Matthew 4:1–11; 2 Corinthians 11:13–14

Every word in the Bible should be applied with proper interpretation.
2 Corinthians 3:6; 1 Timothy 1:3–8; John 8:1–11

Write two of your own "What Does This Mean?" statements for *God's Word Transforms*, along with one or two supporting Scriptures.

-

-

Try to think of one or two other ways the core value *God's Word Transforms* could potentially be misunderstood, along with one or two Scriptures to correct these misunderstandings.

-

-

G

WHAT IS GOD SAYING TO ME?

As you read each of the four core value definitions and supporting scriptures below, take time to wait quietly with the Lord, asking Him, *"What are You saying to me about this core value?"* Use the space below each definition to journal what comes to your mind and spirit as you listen: thoughts, impressions, Scriptures, pictures, etc...

The goal of Scripture is to bring us into a relationship with the Author and transform us into His likeness.

John 5:39–40; 2 Corinthians 3:15–18; James 1:22–25; Ephesians 5:25–27; Psalm 119:11; Luke 24:13–35

"And that from childhood you have known the sacred writings which are able to give you the wisdom that leads to salvation through faith which is in Christ Jesus. All Scripture is inspired by God and profitable for teaching, for reproof, for correction, for training in righteousness; so that the man of God may be adequate, equipped for every good work." - 2 Timothy 3:15–17

"But He answered and said, 'It is written, "Man shall not live on bread alone, but on every word that proceeds out of the mouth of God."'" - Matthew 4:4

As God encounters us in His Word, faith is released into our lives. Studying God's truth empowers us to believe in who He is, who we are, and how He wants us to live.

John 17:17; Matthew 7:24–28; Colossians 3:15–17; John 8:31–32; Psalm 119:105; Romans 15:4; 1 Corinthians 10:1–13; Acts 8:26–40

"So faith comes from hearing, and hearing by the word of Christ." - Romans 10:17

"For this reason we also constantly thank God that when you received the word of God which you heard from us, you accepted it not as the word of men, but for what it really is, the word of God, which also performs its work in you who believe." - 1 Thessalonians 2:13

The primary lens through which we interpret the Bible is the person, life, and redemptive work of Jesus, because He is the most complete revelation of who God is and what God cares about.
Luke 24:25–32; John 1:14, 14:9–11; Colossians 1:15–20, 2:9; Hebrews 1:1–3; 2 Peter 1:16–21

"And the Father who sent Me, He has testified of Me. You have neither heard His voice at any time nor seen His form. You do not have His word abiding in you, for you do not believe Him whom He sent. You search the Scriptures because you think that in them you have eternal life; it is these that testify about Me; and you are unwilling to come to Me so that you may have life. I do not receive glory from men; but I know you, that you do not have the love of God in yourselves. I have come in My Father's name, and you do not receive Me; if another comes in his own name, you will receive him. How can you believe, when you receive glory from one another and you do not seek the glory that is from the one and only God? Do not think that I will accuse you before the Father; the one who accuses you is Moses, in whom you have set your hope. For if you believed Moses, you would believe Me, for he wrote about Me. But if you do not believe his writings, how will you believe My words?" - John 5:37–47

G

The Bible is the source of infallible truth and authority by which we judge all insight and prophetic revelation.
2 Timothy 3:15–17; 2 Thessalonians 2:13–15; 2 Peter 1:16–21; Proverbs 30:5–6; Psalm 119:160; Matthew 4:1–11

"But Jesus answered and said to them, 'You are mistaken, not understanding the Scriptures nor the power of God.'" - Matthew 22:29

"So Jesus was saying to those Jews who had believed Him, 'If you continue in My word, then you are truly disciples of Mine; and you will know the truth, and the truth will make you free.'" - John 8:31–32

ACTIVATIONS

Meditating on God's word leads us into deeper relationship with Him and greater transformation into His likeness. Write out two of your favorite verses and then take five minutes to meditate on each one. As you read, expect the breath of heaven to bring fresh insight and deeper transformation into your life than ever before. Journal or draw a picture of whatever God speaks to your spirit as you meditate on His word.

Think of a subject you'd like to grow in, such as healing the sick, prophecy, the goodness of God, joy, etc., and do a short word search on the topic in your Bible or using an online Bible resource. Choose three verses that are the most meaningful to you and think of a creative way to make these verses become a part of you, such as recording yourself saying them aloud and then listening to them each day this week, or committing them to memory and saying them aloud to yourself three times a day. Take note of the effect this has on your mind and spirit.

TESTIMONIES

"There was a season in my life when I felt the Holy Spirit prompting me to focus on reading the Gospels. Each day I would read a few chapters and meditate on the lifestyle of Jesus and His disciples. As I went deeper into the biblical text, I was overwhelmed with the clear power and authority Christ and His church have been given over the powers of darkness. That next Sunday morning I was charged with expectation. I was excited to pray for people after church and exercise the power I had been reading about. As I prayed, I found myself commanding pain and sickness to go with a unique confidence I hadn't felt in months. One of the ladies I prayed for was instantly healed and I had a fresh awakening in my excitement towards ministry. I was so encouraged to see my Bible reading directly impact my daily life. His words became spirit and life to me personally and to others as I allowed them to move beyond my personal devotional time."

-JARED N.

G

Write one or two stories of times you've seen God's Word transform you or someone you know.

-

-

MY MESSAGE

Whether teaching at a conference or encouraging yourself in the transformative power of God's Word, use this sermon preparation guide to organize your thoughts so you can help yourself and others understand this core value.

My favorite scriptures for this core value:

My interpretation of these scriptures:

Key points I want to communicate:

The key phrase of the testimony I'll share as an example of this core value:

Example of how these truths could be applied to a real life situation:

The change, inspiration, impartation, and/or call to action I want others to embrace after learning that God's Word transforms:

HOW AM I DOING?

Take a few minutes to reread the core value definitions at the beginning of this chapter and then rate yourself from 1–5 in each area below to help you identify strengths and opportunities for growth. Use this information to help you create personal growth goals on the following page.

1 / NEVER **2** / RARELY **3** / SOMETIMES **4** / OFTEN **5** / ALWAYS

I KNOW GOD'S WORD TRANSFORMS

____ I can articulate it.

____ I have experienced it in personal and/or corporate settings.

____ I have a growing affection for it and I desire to apply it.

I DO THIS CORE VALUE

____ I am taking risks and sharing testimonies as I practice this core value.

____ I invite people into my life who exhibit, call out, and give me feedback in this value.

I BELIEVE GOD'S WORD TRANSFORMS

____ I have identified and replaced opposing beliefs and behaviors that hinder my growth in this area.

____ I believe it even when I am alone and no one is watching.

____ My level of hope and expectation has increased in this area.

I REPRODUCE THIS CORE VALUE

____ I have it as a priority in my life.

____ I am intentional in reproducing it in others and can see their progress.

____ I have stories of how others have recognized and been impacted by it in my life.

I AM THIS CORE VALUE

____ I have consistently lived each of the prior stages for many years in a variety of settings.

____ It is my natural response as I make decisions and respond to situations in my everyday life.

____ I understand the spiritual authority I have in this area and intentionally influence those around me.

GROWING IN THIS CORE VALUE

Using your personal assessment from the previous page, ask Holy Spirit to help you write a short-term and long-term goal for each of the following areas. Remember to make your goals time-specific, measurable, and realistic. Choose one to focus on this week and, as you accomplish it, come back and check it off so you can see your growth. Below are some examples to get you started.

MYSELF

- [ ] This week I'll find a Bible study on the book of Philippians and complete it within the next month so I can get a deeper understanding of joy.
- [ ] Short-range goal: ______
- [ ] Long-range goal: ______

MY HOME/FAMILY

- [ ] Within the next two days, I will invite my roommate/family to join me for a three-week Bible study on the goodness of God.
- [ ] Short-range goal: ______
- [ ] Long-range goal: ______

MY PLACE OF WORK/SCHOOL

- [ ] I will ask the Holy Spirit to show me two Scriptures to pray for my city/nation for the next week and then look for the ways in which my prayers are being answered.
- [ ] Short-range goal: ______
- [ ] Long-range goal: ______

OTHER

- [ ] ______
- [ ] ______

NOTES

G

THIS IS THE GOAL
OF PROPHECY: TO CONNECT
PEOPLE TO THE EMPOWERING
NATURE OF GOD SO THEY
CAN BECOME LIKE HIM AND
DISPLAY HIS MARVELOUS
NATURE TO ALL THE EARTH.

SHAWN BOLZ

GOD IS STILL
SPEAKING

GOD IS STILL SPEAKING

DEFINING THE CORE VALUE

God wants to communicate with His family. It is important for us to actively listen for His voice and experience the variety of ways He communicates.
John 10:26–28, 16:13; Matthew 4:4; Isaiah 50:4–5; 1 John 2:27; Acts 2:17; Numbers 11:29; 1 Kings 19:9–13

Scripture calls us to earnestly desire the gift of prophecy, which is to speak on God's behalf to strengthen, encourage, and comfort people. We desire to say what the Father is saying to help people grow in their identity and discover their God-given purpose and value.
1 Corinthians 14:1–4; John 12:49; 1 Timothy 4:14–16; Acts 2:17; 1 Corinthians 14:24–25; Acts 13:1–3

Prophecy is not one-way communication. It involves two people hearing from God: the one who gives the prophetic word and the one who receives it. With the Holy Spirit, Scripture and our community, we judge the spirit and accuracy of the words we give and receive. Holding on to what is good, we let go of what is not.
1 Thessalonians 5:19–22; 1 Corinthians 14:29; Luke 9:55; Acts 21:10–22:24, 27:10, 22–24

The Bible is the ultimate, authoritative revelation unlike any other; nothing will be added to it. Therefore, prophecy should never contradict properly interpreted Scripture.
Galatians 1:6–9; 2 Timothy 3:16–17; 2 Thessalonians 2:13–15; Matthew 7:15–20; John 8:31–32; 2 Peter 1:16–21

WHAT DOES THIS MEAN?

God speaks to us in a variety of ways. We do not make major life decisions solely on the basis of a prophetic word, devoid of other sources of God's leading and communication, such as prayer, Scripture, counsel from mature leaders, covenant relationships, personal desires, etc.

John 10:27–28; 2 Timothy 3:16–17; James 1:5–6; Proverbs 24:6; Acts 11

God is perfect, but He has chosen to partner with imperfect people to build the Kingdom. Like other spiritual gifts, such as teaching, leading and serving, we do not always prophesy perfectly. We sometimes make mistakes and this is why we need to judge the words.

1 Corinthians 13:9–12; 1 Thessalonians 5:19–21; 1 Corinthians 14:29–33; 1 Corinthians 12:4–11; Amos 3:7; Romans 12:6–10; Acts 15:28

As with all spiritual gifts, the gift of prophecy is not given to us fully developed. We are responsible to grow and develop our gifts to their full potential by stepping out in faith, taking risks, and partnering with God.

1 Timothy 4:14–16; 2 Timothy 1:6; 1 Corinthians 14:1–3; 1 Corinthians 14:12

God often speaks to us in the language of our own mind and spirit. Therefore, the voice of the Lord often sounds like us but is smarter than us. We practice to discern His voice with confidence.

1 Corinthians 2:12–16; Psalm 16:7; John 10:14–16,27; Isaiah 30:21; Acts 16:7–10

In the Old Testament the prophet is judged, but in the New Testament the prophetic word is judged. The Old Testament expectation that all prophecy should be 100% accurate has been modified under the New Covenant. The New Testament church is commanded to test everything and hold on to what is good. In the Old Testament, the Spirit was only upon the prophet. Now the Holy Spirit resides in every believer, enabling us to say "You got that wrong," instead of "You are a false prophet."

1 Thessalonians 5:19–21; 1 Corinthians 14:29; 1 John 4:1; Acts 2:17–18; Deuteronomy 18:18–22

WHAT DOES THIS MEAN? (CONTINUED)

Giving inaccurate words of edification and encouragement does not make someone a false prophet. In the New Testament, false prophets are largely defined as people who teach wrong doctrine, produce bad fruit, and perform signs and wonders designed to deceive.

2 Peter 2:1–3; Matthew 7:15–23; Matthew 24:24; 2 Timothy 4:3–4; 1 Corinthians 14:3

Prophecy should always be delivered with humility and love, never for self-promotion or selfish ambition. If we give an inaccurate word or do so with a wrong heart, we take responsibility for our mistake, repent and reconcile with those affected.

Philippians 2:3–4; 1 Corinthians 13:1–2; Colossians 3:13–15

Prophecy is a three-part process of revelation, interpretation, and application. Just like Scripture, prophecy can be misunderstood, misinterpreted, or poorly applied.

1 Corinthians 14:29–31; Acts 10:9–16, 21:10–22:30, 27:10, 22–24

We do not force prophecy to be fulfilled out of season. Rather, we wait in faith for His timing and His way, co-laboring with God as needed.

Genesis 15:2–5, 16:1–2, 21:2; Habakkuk 2:2–3; Hebrews 6:12; 2 Kings 5:10–14; Acts 9:1–19

There is sometimes a mystery to prophecy and its timing. Some prophetic words are beyond anything we've ever thought or imagined, and can only be understood in hindsight, so we hold on to them for a later time.

Luke 1:31–34, 24:44–45; John 13:7, 16:12

DO NOT MISUNDERSTAND

We don't always prophesy perfectly.

1 Corinthians 14:29; 1 Thessalonians 5:19–22

No one person has full revelation or understanding. Therefore, we should submit revelation for feedback from the Christian community.

1 Corinthians 2:16, 12:7–12, 14:26–30,

We are accountable for the prophetic words we give and are committed to growing in accuracy.

Matthew 12:36–37; 1 Peter 4:10–11; 1 Corinthians 14:26–30

Prophetic words are not the only way to know the heart and will of God.

Hebrews 8:10; 2 Timothy 3:16–17; Romans 12:2

As trusted children, we do not have to check with God on everything we do, like what clothes to wear or what street to walk down. However, He does sometimes have ideas about these, things which can lead us to an adventure.

Acts 16:7–9; 1 Corinthians 10:27–31; Mark 11:1–6; Luke 22:8–12

Prophets and prophecy do not have to look or feel weird to be from God.

1 Corinthians 14:3, 23–28, 39-40

It is still important for us to learn from biblically sound teachers and to study Scripture.

Ephesians 4:11–13; 1 Corinthians 12:28; 2 Timothy 3:16; Acts 17:11; Matthew 28:18–20

Write two of your own "What Does This Mean?" statements for the core value *God is Still Speaking*, along with one or two supporting Scriptures.

-

-

Try to think of one or two other ways the core value *God is Still Speaking* could potentially be misunderstood, along with one or two Scriptures to correct these misunderstandings.

-

-

WHAT IS GOD SAYING TO ME?

As you read each of the four core value definitions and supporting scriptures below, take time to wait quietly with the Lord, asking Him, *"What are You saying to me about this core value?"* Use the space below each definition to journal what comes to your mind and spirit as you listen: thoughts, impressions, Scriptures, pictures, etc...

God wants to communicate with His family. It is important for us to actively listen for His voice and experience the variety of ways He communicates.
Matthew 4:4; Isaiah 50:4–5; 1 John 2:27; Acts 2:17; Numbers 11:29; 1 Kings 19:9–13

"But you do not believe because you are not of My sheep. My sheep hear My voice, and I know them, and they follow Me; and I give eternal life to them, and they will never perish; and no one will snatch them out of My hand." - John 10:26–28

"But when He, the Spirit of truth, comes, He will guide you into all the truth; for He will not speak on His own initiative, but whatever He hears, He will speak; and He will disclose to you what is to come." - John 16:13

Scripture calls us to earnestly desire the gift of prophecy, which is to speak on God's behalf to strengthen, encourage, and comfort people. We desire to say what the Father is saying in order to help others grow in their identity and discover their God-given purpose and value.
John 12:49; 1 Timothy 4:14–16; Acts 2:17; 1 Corinthians 14:24–25; Acts 13:1–3

"Pursue love, yet desire earnestly spiritual gifts, but especially that you may prophesy. For one who speaks in a tongue does not speak to men but to God; for no one understands, but in his spirit he speaks mysteries. But one who prophesies speaks to men for edification and exhortation and consolation. One who speaks in a tongue edifies himself; but one who prophesies edifies the church."
- 1 Corinthians 14:1–4

Prophecy is not one-way communication. It involves two people hearing from God: the one who gives the prophetic word and the one who receives it. With the Holy Spirit, Scripture, and our community, we judge the spirit and accuracy of the words we give and receive. Holding on to what is good, we let go of what is not.
1 Corinthians 14:29; Acts 21:10–22:24, 27:10, 22–24

"Do not quench the Spirit; do not despise prophetic utterances. But examine everything carefully; hold fast to that which is good; abstain from every form of evil." - 1 Thessalonians 5:19–22

"But He turned and rebuked them, and said, 'You do not know what kind of spirit you are of; for the Son of Man did not come to destroy men's lives, but to save them.' And they went on to another village." - Luke 9:55

The Bible is the ultimate, authoritative revelation unlike any other; nothing will be added to it. Therefore, prophecy should never contradict properly interpreted Scripture.
Galatians 1:6–9; 2 Thessalonians 2:13–15; Matthew 7:15–20; John 8:31–32; 2 Peter 1:16–21

"All Scripture is inspired by God and profitable for teaching, for reproof, for correction, for training in righteousness; so that the man of God may be adequate, equipped for every good work."
- 2 Timothy 3:16–17

"So Jesus was saying to those Jews who had believed Him, 'If you continue in My word, then you are truly disciples of Mine; and you will know the truth, and the truth will make you free.'" - John 8:31–32

ACTIVATIONS

God wants to speak to us and through us in many creative ways. Take a few minutes to sit with the Lord and experiment increasing your ability to hear and recognize His voice through your senses: feeling, hearing, seeing, tasting, and smelling. Ask the Holy Spirit to give you a prophetic encouragement, exhortation, or comforting word for five different people, using each of your five senses. In the boxes below, write the names of the people whom you want to encourage and then the prophetic word you have for them.

	PERSON'S NAME	PROPHETIC WORD	IMPACT OF THE WORD
SEE			
FEEL			
HEAR			
TASTE			
SMELL			

G

God loves to talk to His children. Sometimes when He is speaking you will hear a song in your head or see a short clip from a movie run through your imagination. God is timeless, so He is aware of today's movies, books and songs. Spend a few quiet moments with your Father and ask Him what He wants to speak to you personally. Let Him sing a song over you, or quote a line from one of your favorite movies. Journal whatever you hear from Him and ask Him to explain what it means for you.

TESTIMONIES

"My kids love playing together in the park. There is always laughter and fun. I usually join them but on this particularly gray winter day a lady caught my eye and I immediately knew God wanted to speak to her. 'Hey, guys!' I said. 'Come here for a minute.' I had taught my six and eight year old how to listen to God and speak His words of encouragement to each other at home but they had never done it with a stranger. When I explained what I believed God wanted to do they were excited. After a quick prayer, they heard what He wanted to say to the woman. With nervous excitement we all approached her. Zak confidently shared his words first, followed by Rosie and then me. She started crying immediately. What we said was exactly what she was going through. She shared her pain and we were honored to pray with her and show her God's enormous love for her. She was extremely touched and said she would like to come to church with us. It was a beautiful thing to see her mascara run down her face as she experienced God's love through my kids."

-JONNY G.

G

Write one or two testimonies of a time when you or someone you know were impacted by God speaking.

-

-

MY MESSAGE

Whether you're talking with a Buddhist couple you recently met or preaching in a village in east Africa, use this sermon preparation guide to organize your thoughts so you can help others understand that God is still speaking.

My favorite scriptures for this core value:

My interpretation of these scriptures:

Key points I want to communicate:

The key phrase of the testimony I'll share as an example of this core value:

Example of how these truths could be applied to a real-life situation:

The change, inspiration, impartation, and/or call to action I want others to embrace after learning that God is still speaking:

HOW AM I DOING?

Take a few minutes to reread the core value definitions at the beginning of this chapter and then rate yourself from 1–5 in each area below to help you identify strengths and opportunities for growth. Use this information to help you create personal growth goals on the following page.

1 / NEVER **2** / RARELY **3** / SOMETIMES **4** / OFTEN **5** / ALWAYS

I KNOW GOD IS STILL SPEAKING

____ I can articulate it.

____ I can identify it in Scripture, books, movies, testimonies, sermons, and life.

____ I have experienced it in personal and/or corporate settings.

I DO THIS CORE VALUE

____ I am taking risks and sharing testimonies as I practice this core value.

____ I invite people into my life who exhibit, call out, and give me feedback in this value.

I BELIEVE GOD IS STILL SPEAKING

____ I have identified and replaced opposing beliefs and behaviors that hinder my growth in this area.

____ My level of hope and expectation has increased in this area.

____ I usually view and respond to life through the lens of it.

I REPRODUCE THIS CORE VALUE

____ I bring the strength of it as I serve others and build community.

____ I am intentional in reproducing it in others and can see their progress.

____ I have stories of how others have recognized and been impacted by it in my life.

I AM THIS CORE VALUE

____ I am an innovator, explorer, and articulator of it and people seek my wisdom concerning it.

____ I naturally multiply it. I can identify people whom I have taught and are now effectively teaching others to live this core value.

____ I understand the spiritual authority I have in this area and intentionally influence those around me.

G

GROWING IN THIS CORE VALUE

Using your personal assessment from the previous page, ask Holy Spirit to help you write a short-term and long-term goal for each of the following areas. Remember to make your goals time-specific, measurable, and realistic. Choose one to focus on this week and, as you accomplish it, come back and check it off so you can see your growth. Below are some examples to get you started.

MYSELF

- ☐ Today I will ask the Holy Spirit for a Scripture to encourage someone. Then I will draw a picture or write a note to go with it and then ask the Holy Spirit to show me who to give it to.
- ☐ Short-range goal: ____________________
- ☐ Long-range goal: ____________________

MY HOME/FAMILY

- ☐ I will prophesy over each of my family members or housemates before the end of the week and ask them to give me feedback to help me grow in prophecy.
- ☐ Short-range goal: ____________________
- ☐ Long-range goal: ____________________

MY PLACE OF WORK/SCHOOL

- ☐ Within the next two days, I will take a risk and practice covert prophecy at work/school. I will listen and say what the Father is saying, without using Christian language, to help one of my coworkers/classmates grow in their identity and God-given purpose.
- ☐ Short-range goal: ____________________
- ☐ Long-range goal: ____________________

OTHER

- ☐ ____________________
- ☐ ____________________

NOTES

G

FEAR LOOKS;

FAITH JUMPS. FAITH

NEVER FAILS TO

OBTAIN ITS OBJECT.

IF I LEAVE YOU AS

I FOUND YOU, I AM NOT

GOD'S CHANNEL.

SMITH WIGGLESWORTH

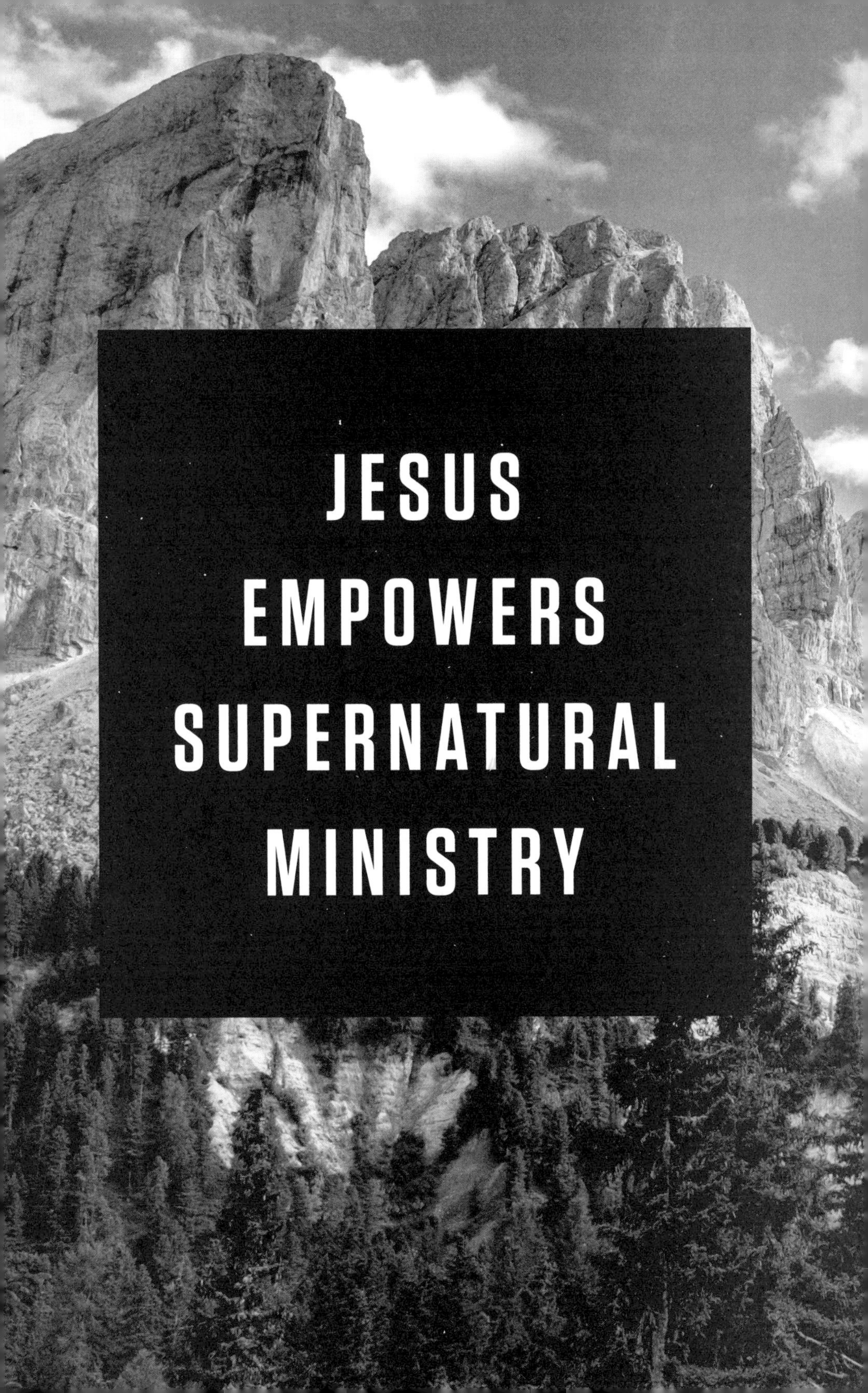
JESUS
EMPOWERS
SUPERNATURAL
MINISTRY

JESUS EMPOWERS SUPERNATURAL MINISTRY

DEFINING THE CORE VALUE

Jesus promised signs would follow believers and they would do even greater works than He did.
John 14:12–14; Acts 2:17–18; Luke 9:1–2; Mark 16:15–18; Acts 5:12–16

We owe the world an opportunity to experience the power of God and an invitation to salvation because Jesus sent us into the world, just as the Father sent Him, with the power of the Holy Spirit.
John 20:21–23; 1 Corinthians 2:4–5; John 17:18; 1 Thessalonians 1:5; Matthew 28:18–19, 5:14–16; Luke 10:1–9

Nothing is impossible with God. Therefore, no person or situation is beyond His ability to bring complete restoration.
Matthew 17:20; Mark 10:25–27; John 15:7; 1 Corinthians 6:9–11; Psalm 103:1–7; Luke 1:34–37

We believe all can be healed because Jesus demonstrated the Father's will in healing all the sick and demonized He encountered.
Matthew 4:23, 12:15, 14:14, 24–33; Luke 9:11; Acts 10:38; Psalm 103:3–4; Acts 3:1–10; James 2:14–18; Mark 10:46–52; Matthew 9:27–38

WHAT DOES THIS MEAN?

Miracles did not stop with Jesus and the apostles.
Hebrews 13:8; 1 John 4:17; Mark 16:17–18; Acts 2:38–39; 1 Corinthians 14:1, 39; 1 Peter 4:7, 10; 2 Timothy 1:6–8

The cross of Jesus does not simply make us good people; it creates a new kind of people who walk in His power and are naturally supernatural.
2 Corinthians 5:17; 1 Peter 2:9–12; 2 Peter 1:3–4; Mark 16:17–18

The Holy Spirit gives every believer the supernatural power to witness and release miracles, signs, and wonders.
John 14:12; Acts 1:8, 2:16–18; 1 Corinthians 12:7–11, 2:4–5, 4:20; Matthew 10:8; John 20:21–23

Love should be our primary motivation when we take risks to release the power of God's Kingdom into the lives of others.
1 Corinthians 16:14, 13:1–3; Galatians 5:13; John 13:34–35; Matthew 20:26–28

We walk as sons and daughters of God, revealing our Father's goodness and calling others to repentance.
1 Peter 2:9–12; 2 Corinthians 5:17–20; Matthew 11:25–30

Our new normal is to live a Spirit-led life and assist in establishing God's Kingdom on earth.
Acts 1:6–8, 13:1–5; John 5:19

Injustice and works of darkness are an opportunity for God's supernatural love and power to move through us.
Romans 5:20; 1 John 3:8, 4:18; Psalm 23:4–5; 1 John 4:4; Matthew 10:16–20, 16:19

The Father wants us to live in the fullness of the Kingdom, which means that we are to be persistent in prayer, waiting in faith for the Kingdom to break into every situation.
John 10:10; Luke 18:1–8, 11:1–13, 12:31–32; Acts 1:4, 2:1–4, 4:23–31

WHAT DOES THIS MEAN? (CONTINUED)

We celebrate every victory, great and small, believing that every testimony of what Jesus has done creates faith and releases hope that He will do it again. In this way, a testimony is a prophecy of what Jesus is willing and able to do right now.
Revelation 19:10; Romans 10:15–17; Hebrews 13:7–8; Acts 10:34-48; Psalm 44:1–5; Mark 5:18–21; Psalm 119:111; Deuteronomy 6:17–24, 7:17–19; Revelation 12:10–11

DO NOT MISUNDERSTAND

We are not Jesus.
Colossians 1:15–20, 27; Philippians 2:6–11; Acts 3:12

We do not pursue a relationship with God just so that we can perform signs and wonders.
Luke 10:17–20; Matthew 7:21–23

Miracles are an expression of the love and power of God, not an indication that we are more important in the Kingdom.
1 Corinthians 13:1–3; Matthew 7:21–23

If, in our passion and enthusiasm to minister, we accidentally hurt or dishonor someone, we are quick to take responsibility and humbly apologize.
Philippians 2:3–4; Colossians 3:12–14; Ephesians 4:2–3; 1 Corinthians 13:4–8

We do not have to strive for the grace needed to operate in signs and wonders.
Galatians 3:2–5; 1 Corinthians 15:10; Ephesians 3:7–9

The risks we take when ministering do not always result in the expected outcome.
Acts 16:16–24; Matthew 14:22–33; Romans 8:28

We will experience resistance to the gospel and persecution as we seek to follow Christ.
Acts 4:3–22, 5:12–42; Revelation 12:10–11; 2 Corinthians 11:24–25; Matthew 5:10; 2 Corinthians 4:7–12

Write two of your own "What Does This Mean?" statements for *Jesus Empowers Supernatural Ministry*, along with one or two supporting Scriptures.

-

-

Try to think of one or two other ways the core value *Jesus Empowers Supernatural Ministry* could potentially be misunderstood, along with one or two Scriptures to correct these misunderstandings.

-

-

J

WHAT IS GOD SAYING TO ME?

As you read each of the four core value definitions and supporting scriptures below, take time to wait quietly with the Lord, asking Him, *"What are You saying to me about this core value?"* Use the space below each definition to journal what comes to your mind and spirit as you listen: thoughts, impressions, Scriptures, pictures, etc...

Jesus promised signs would follow believers and they would do even greater works than He did.
Acts 2:17–18; Luke 9:1–2; Mark 16:15–18; Acts 5:12–16

"Truly, truly, I say to you, he who believes in Me, the works that I do, he will do also; and greater works than these he will do, because I go to My Father. Whatever you ask in My name, that I will do, so that the Father may be glorified in the Son. If you ask anything in My name, I will do it."
- John 14:12–14

We owe the world an opportunity to experience the power of God and an invitation to salvation because Jesus sent us into the world, just as the Father sent Him, with the power of the Holy Spirit.
John 17:18; 1 Thessalonians 1:5; Matthew 28:18–19, 5:14–16; Luke 10:1–9

"So Jesus said to them again, 'Peace be with you; as the Father has sent Me, I also send you.'"
- John 20:21–23

"And my message and my preaching were not in persuasive words of wisdom, but in demonstration of the Spirit and of power, so that your faith would not rest on the wisdom of men, but on the power of God." - 1 Corinthians 2:4–5

Nothing is impossible with God. Therefore, no person or situation is beyond His ability to bring complete restoration.
John 15:7; 1 Corinthians 6:9–11; Psalm 103:1–7; Luke 1:34–37

"And He said to them, 'Because of the littleness of your faith; for truly I say to you, if you have faith the size of a mustard seed, you will say to this mountain, "Move from here to there," and it will move; and nothing will be impossible to you.'" - Matthew 17:20

"'It is easier for a camel to go through the eye of a needle than for a rich man to enter the Kingdom of God.' They were even more astonished and said to Him, 'Then who can be saved?' Looking at them, Jesus said, 'With people it is impossible, but not with God; for all things are possible with God.'" - Mark 10:25–27

We believe all can be healed because Jesus demonstrated the Father's will in healing all the sick and demonized He encountered.
Matthew 14:14, 24–33; Luke 9:11; Acts 10:38; Psalm 103:3–4; Acts 3:1–10; James 2:14–18; Mark 10:46–52; Matthew 9:27–38

"Jesus was going throughout all Galilee, teaching in their synagogues and proclaiming the gospel of the Kingdom, and healing every kind of disease and every kind of sickness among the people."
- Matthew 4:23

"But Jesus, aware of this, withdrew from there. Many followed Him, and He healed them all."
- Matthew 12:15

J

ACTIVATIONS

If you have access to the internet, visit the Bethel.TV YouTube channel and watch two or three testimonies of God's supernatural healing power to help your hunger and faith grow and to expand your perspective of what is possible. Record your thoughts.

Ask God to help you think of one or two people operating in a higher level of supernatural power than you and ask if you can spend time ministering with them and learning from them. Write down the names of the people God shows you.

Pray for boldness and ask God to give you an opportunity to lead someone to Christ. Record your testimony below.

TESTIMONIES

"My wife and I were having dinner at a busy restaurant in Redding. As we spoke with our waitress, Anna, I had a simple prophetic word for her. I told her God had a plan for her to travel in the future, potentially even work in the airline industry. She began to open up and share about the crises she had been through over the last year. My wife and I shared the gospel with her and told her Jesus heals the brokenhearted. I told Anna that if she comes to Him, He will heal her heart and wipe her slate clean. She cried as I told her the parable of the prodigal son. With tears in her eyes she said, 'That's amazing.' When we gave her opportunity to pray and dedicate her life to Jesus she knelt down at our dinner table of her own accord. Although the restaurant was full and there were people all around, on bended-knee, with eyes closed, Anna prayed and received Jesus into her heart."

-MATT K.

Write two stories of times you saw Jesus empower supernatural ministry in your life or someone else's life.

-

-

J

MY MESSAGE

Whether preaching to thousands in a stadium or chatting with friends online, use this sermon preparation guide to organize your thoughts so you can help others understand that Jesus empowers supernatural ministry.

My favorite scriptures for this core value:

My interpretation of these scriptures:

Key points I want to communicate:

The key phrase of the testimony I'll share as an example of this core value:

Example of how these truths could be applied to a real-life situation:

The change, inspiration, impartation, and/or call to action I want others to embrace after learning that Jesus empowers supernatural ministry:

HOW AM I DOING?

Take a few minutes to reread the core value definitions at the beginning of this chapter and then rate yourself from 1–5 in each area below to help you identify strengths and opportunities for growth. Use this information to help you create personal growth goals on the following page.

1 / NEVER **2** / RARELY **3** / SOMETIMES **4** / OFTEN **5** / ALWAYS

I KNOW JESUS EMPOWERS SUPERNATURAL MINISTRY

____ I can articulate it.

____ I can identify it in Scripture, books, movies, testimonies, sermons, and life.

____ I have experienced it in personal and/or corporate settings.

I DO THIS CORE VALUE

____ I am taking risks and sharing testimonies as I practice this core value.

____ I invite people into my life who exhibit, call out, and give me feedback in this value.

I BELIEVE JESUS EMPOWERS SUPERNATURAL MINISTRY

____ I believe it even when I am alone and no one is watching.

____ My level of hope and expectation has increased in this area.

____ I usually view and respond to life through the lens of it.

I REPRODUCE THIS CORE VALUE

____ I have it as a priority in my life.

____ I am intentionally reproducing it in others and can see their progress.

____ I have stories of how others have recognized and been impacted by it in my life.

I AM THIS CORE VALUE

____ I have consistently lived each of the prior stages for many years in a variety of settings.

____ I am an innovator, explorer, and articulator of it and people seek my wisdom concerning it.

____ I naturally multiply it. I can identify people whom I have taught and are now effectively teaching others to live this core value.

J

GROWING IN THIS CORE VALUE

Using your personal assessment from the previous page, ask Holy Spirit to help you write a short-term and long-term goal for each of the following areas. Remember to make your goals time-specific, measurable, and realistic. Choose one to focus on this week and, as you accomplish it, come back and check it off so you can see your growth. Below are some examples to get you started.

MYSELF

- ☐ Right now, I will write down two practical steps to take so I can grow in supernatural ministry. For example, I will ask a friend to step out in faith with me to pray for healing for someone.
- ☐ Short-range goal: ____________________
- ☐ Long-range goal: ____________________

MY HOME/FAMILY

- ☐ I will intentionally look for three opportunities to reproduce the truth that Jesus empowers supernatural ministry with my family/roommates this week.
- ☐ Short-range goal: ____________________
- ☐ Long-range goal: ____________________

MY PLACE OF WORK/SCHOOL

- ☐ Today I will spend 30 minutes dreaming with the Holy Spirit about the "greater works" Jesus tells us about in John 14:12 and how I can live out this Scripture this week at work or school.
- ☐ Short-range goal: ____________________
- ☐ Long-range goal: ____________________

OTHER

- ☐ ____________________

NOTES

J

J

THE KINGDOM

DOES NOT PRIMARILY

ADVANCE THROUGH

INFILTRATION

OR INVASION BUT

BY INVITATION.

KRIS VALLOTTON

HIS KINGDOM IS ADVANCING

HIS KINGDOM IS ADVANCING

DEFINING THE CORE VALUE

God is big and victorious. The devil is small and defeated. We are in a battle, but the outcome is not in doubt!
1 John 4:4; Colossians 2:13–15; 1 John 2:13, 5:4–5; Romans 8:31–39; John 12:31; Acts 4:23–31; 1 John 3:8; Hebrews 2:14–15; John 16:33: Mark 5:1–13

We believe and live the prayer, "Your Kingdom come, Your will be done on earth as it is in heaven." Therefore, we partner with the King in natural and supernatural ways to establish mercy, justice, and righteousness until He comes.
Matthew 6:9–10, 10:7–8; Isaiah 9:7, 33:5–6; Micah 6:8; Matthew 10:42, 25:40; John 14:12; James 1:27; Matthew 12:22–29

As believers, we are all in full-time ministry as God advances His Kingdom into every area of society. Our work and efforts both inside and outside the church are sacred and valuable acts of worship to God.
1 Peter 2:9; Romans 12:1; Matthew 5:13–16; Colossians 3:23–24; Daniel 6:3; Proverbs 22:29; Ephesians 6:5–9; Matthew 25:31–46

Although we will experience resistance and conflict as the Kingdom advances, we expect the culture to be changed as people come to salvation and take their places in God's purpose for the world.
John 15:19–21, 16:33; Colossians 1:13–14; 2 Corinthians 4:8–11, 12:10; Nehemiah 2:1–10; Matthew 5:13–16; Acts 19:11–41

WHAT DOES THIS MEAN?

We focus on the good God is doing in the world and live with contagious hope and joy.
Romans 15:13; 2 Corinthians 4:16–18; Philippians 4:8–9; Ephesians 1:17–19; Acts 13:52

Jesus has already won; we pray and minister from the power of His victory over darkness.
Ephesians 1:18–23, 2:4–6; 1 John 3:8, 4:4; Matthew 11:11; Isaiah 54:17

We recognize that God's Spirit is at work everywhere in the world and we partner with Him so people are reconciled to Him.
Psalm 139:7; Romans 5:20; 2 Corinthians 5:16–20; Matthew 10:7–8; Mark 16:15–18; Romans 10:14–15; Colossians 1:28–29; Matthew 24:14

We seek heaven's answers for earthly problems and take practical risks in faith to see these answers realized in our world.
Matthew 6:9–10; Genesis 41:1–46; Acts 11:27–30; Matthew 17:24–27; 1 Samuel 14:6–23; Acts 3:1–10

We discover our gifts and excel in them in order to best serve society and its leaders, so we all may prosper.
Daniel 1:16–21, 2:26–28; Genesis 41:1–46; 1 Timothy 2:1–2; 1 Peter 4:10–11; 1 Timothy 4:14–16; Proverbs 22:29; Exodus 31:1–11

We bless and pray for people who persecute us as we seek to bring heaven to earth.
Matthew 5:43–45; Luke 6:27–28; Proverbs 25:21; Acts 16:22–34

One of the ways we transform the world is by agreeing with and declaring the good news of the Kingdom.
Proverbs 11:11; 2 Corinthians 4:13; Matthew 10:7–8; Proverbs 18:21; James 3:2–5; Matthew 16:18–19, 18:18–20, 21:21–22

We live to make the world better for future generations that we may never see.
Proverbs 13:22; Deuteronomy 7:9; 2 Timothy 2:2; Isaiah 9:7

DO NOT MISUNDERSTAND

Even though we live with hope, we do not deny the existence of difficult or painful circumstances.
John 16:33; 2 Corinthians 4:7–11, 16–18; 1 Corinthians 4:11–13; Philippians 4:11–14

The enemy will try to resist us and we will experience opposition and persecution.
2 Timothy 3:12; Romans 8:31–39; Acts 14:22–23; 1 Thessalonians 2:17–18; Philippians 1:12–14

We cannot change the world by human strength and ability alone.
Zechariah 4:6; 2 Corinthians 3:4–6; Jeremiah 17:5–6; 1 Peter 4:10–11

While we hope everyone will be reconciled to God, sadly, not all will respond to the invitation to come home to the Father.
Matthew 22:1–14, 13:24–30; 1 Timothy 2:3–5; 2 Peter 3:9; Matthew 25:31–46

God desires to prosper and bless leaders in society so that society itself will be a blessing.
1 Timothy 2:1–2; Jeremiah 29:7; Isaiah 60:1–3; 61:1–4; Proverbs 11:11; Jonah 3

We do not have to be at the highest point of influence in society to bring Kingdom changes.
Luke 13:18–21; Matthew 20:25–27; Acts 4:13; Genesis 41:1–41

A lifestyle of servanthood is often the means by which we gain greater favor and influence in society.
Matthew 20:25–27; Philippians 2:5–18; Luke 2:51–52; 1 Samuel 2:26; Daniel 2:1–49

Some aspects of the Kingdom that we are pursuing may not be witnessed in our lifetime, but rather in the lives of our children's children.
Hebrews 11:13; Philippians 3:13–14; 1 Corinthians 9:24

Write two of your own "What Does This Mean?" statements for *His Kingdom is Advancing*, along with one or two supporting Scriptures.

-
-

Try to think of one or two other ways the core value *His Kingdom is Advancing* could potentially be misunderstood, along with one or two Scriptures to correct these misunderstandings.

-
-

H

WHAT IS GOD SAYING TO ME?

As you read each of the four core value definitions and supporting scriptures below, take time to wait quietly with the Lord, asking Him, *"What are You saying to me about this core value?"* Use the space below each definition to journal what comes to your mind and spirit as you listen: thoughts, impressions, Scriptures, pictures, etc...

God is big and victorious. The devil is small and defeated. We are in a battle, but the outcome is not in doubt!
1 John 2:13, 3:8, 5:4–5; Romans 8:31–39; John 12:31; Acts 4:23–31; Hebrews 2:14–15; Mark 5:1–13

"You are from God, little children, and have overcome them; because greater is He who is in you than he who is in the world." - 1 John 4:4

"When you were dead in your transgressions and the uncircumcision of your flesh, He made you alive together with Him, having forgiven us all our transgressions, having canceled out the certificate of debt consisting of decrees against us, which was hostile to us; and He has taken it out of the way, having nailed it to the cross. When He had disarmed the rulers and authorities, He made a public display of them, having triumphed over them through Him." - Colossians 2:13–15

We believe and live the prayer, "Your Kingdom come, Your will be done on earth as it is in heaven." Therefore, we partner with the King in natural and supernatural ways to establish mercy, justice, and righteousness until He comes.
Isaiah 9:7, 33:5–6; Micah 6:8; Matthew 10:42, 12:22–29, 25:40; John 14:12; James 1:27

"Pray, then, in this way: 'Our Father who is in heaven, Hallowed be Your name. Your Kingdom come. Your will be done, On earth as it is in heaven.'" - Matthew 6:9–10

"These things I have spoken to you, so that in Me you may have peace. In the world you have tribulation, but take courage; I have overcome the world." - Matthew 10:7–8

As believers, we are all in full-time ministry as God advances His Kingdom into every area of society. Our work and efforts both inside and outside the church are sacred and valuable acts of worship to God.

Matthew 5:13–16, 25:31–46; Colossians 3:23–24; Daniel 6:3; Proverbs 22:29; Ephesians 6:5–9

"But you are a chosen race, a royal priesthood, a holy nation, a people for God's own possession, so that you may proclaim the excellencies of Him who has called you out of darkness into His marvelous light." - 1 Peter 2:9

"Therefore I urge you, brethren, by the mercies of God, to present your bodies a living and holy sacrifice, acceptable to God, which is your spiritual service of worship." - Romans 12:1

Although we will experience resistance and conflict as the Kingdom advances, we expect the culture to be changed as people come to salvation and take their places in God's purpose for the world.

Colossians 1:13–14; 2 Corinthians 4:8–11, 12:10; Nehemiah 2:1–10; Matthew 5:13–16; Acts 19:11–41

"If you were of the world, the world would love its own; but because you are not of the world, but I chose you out of the world, because of this the world hates you. Remember the word that I said to you, 'A slave is not greater than his master.' If they persecuted Me, they will also persecute you; if they kept My word, they will keep yours also. But all these things they will do to you for My name's sake, because they do not know the One who sent Me." - John 15:19–21

"These things I have spoken to you, so that in Me you may have peace. In the world you have tribulation, but take courage; I have overcome the world." - John 16:33

ACTIVATIONS

To advance God's Kingdom, we need to pray seemingly impossible prayers, such as praying for mass salvations and seeing inner city gang violence cease in a major city in your nation. This can seem impossible to us, but we know with God all things are possible! Take a few moments to write out three seemingly impossible prayers, then spend time praying and imagining with God what these situations will be like when your prayers become reality.

Whatever we focus our thoughts on becomes magnified to us. By focusing on our victories and breakthroughs, we can actually build momentum in our lives and make the voice of our victories louder than the voice of defeat. Below, make a list of areas where you've had victories and seen growth, either big or small, over the last two years. After you make your list, take time to celebrate yourself and what God has done in you!

TESTIMONIES

"Two years ago, I was sitting in my chair during worship and God told me, 'I have anointed you for ministry in business and the church.' I was shocked because I had no business experience. A few months later a friend walked into my office and said, 'Hey, have you seen this business?' As I looked at their website I couldn't believe what I was reading! It was a large international investment company changing the world. They were healing whole countries of diseases and they were Christians! As I read about the directors, my immediate thought was, 'We need to encourage these guys!' I asked some friends to write prophetic words for them and then mailed them off. We couldn't believe what God did next. When the CEO opened his package he began to sob after reading just the first line. As the directors read the prophetic words, God began to move in each of their lives. Their business experienced tremendous financial blessing, making more money in the next three weeks than in the three years prior. This experience moved them so much they flew to Redding to visit Bethel and I had the privilege to watch as 15 children led them again to tears, prophesying and calling out their greatness in specific detail and power. I never thought I would minister to business people, however, God has continued to open many more opportunities. His kingdom is advancing!"

-DAVE H.

Write a story of a time when you saw His Kingdom advancing in your life or the life of someone you know.

H

MY MESSAGE

Whether you're talking to members of your business community or chatting with your neighbor, use this sermon preparation guide to organize your thoughts so you can help others understand that His Kingdom is advancing.

My favorite scriptures for this core value:

My interpretation of these scriptures:

Key points I want to communicate:

The key phrase of the testimony I'll share as an example of this core value:

Example of how these truths could be applied to a real-life situation:

The change, inspiration, impartation, and/or call to action I want others to embrace after learning that God's kingdom is advancing:

HOW AM I DOING?

Take a few minutes to reread the core value definitions at the beginning of this chapter and then rate yourself from 1–5 in each area below to help you identify strengths and opportunities for growth. Use this information to help you create personal growth goals on the following page.

1 / NEVER **2** / RARELY **3** / SOMETIMES **4** / OFTEN **5** / ALWAYS

I KNOW HIS KINGDOM IS ADVANCING

___ I can articulate it.

___ I can identify it in Scripture, books, movies, testimonies, sermons, and life.

___ I have a growing affection for it and I desire to apply it.

I DO THIS CORE VALUE

___ I am taking risks and sharing testimonies as I practice this core value.

___ I invite people into my life who exhibit, call out, and give me feedback in this value.

I BELIEVE HIS KINGDOM IS ADVANCING

___ I have identified and replaced opposing beliefs and behaviors that hinder my growth in this area.

___ My level of hope and expectation has increased in this area.

___ I usually view and respond to life through the lens of it.

I REPRODUCE THIS CORE VALUE

___ I bring the strength of it as I serve others and build community.

___ I am intentionally reproducing it in others and can see their progress.

___ I have stories of how others have recognized and been impacted by it in my life.

I AM THIS CORE VALUE

___ I have consistently lived each of the prior stages for many years in a variety of settings.

___ I naturally multiply it. I can identify people whom I have taught and are now effectively teaching others to live this core value.

___ I understand the spiritual authority I have in this area and intentionally influence those around me.

H

GROWING IN THIS CORE VALUE

Using your personal assessment from the previous page, ask Holy Spirit to help you write a short-term and long-term goal for each of the following areas. Remember to make your goals time-specific, measurable, and realistic. Choose one to focus on this week and, as you accomplish it, come back and check it off so you can see your growth. Below are some examples to get you started.

MYSELF

- ☐ Today I will ask God to show me two people or situations where I can help His Kingdom advance and I will act on whatever He shows me.
- ☐ Short-range goal: ____________________
- ☐ Long-range goal: ____________________

MY HOME/FAMILY

- ☐ My family and I will ask the Holy Spirit to show us any areas where we are believing the lie that the devil is bigger than God. We will then ask the Holy Spirit what the truth is, write it down, and put it some place prominent in our house and declare it together every day this week.
- ☐ Short-range goal: ____________________
- ☐ Long-range goal: ____________________

MY PLACE OF WORK/SCHOOL

- ☐ Over the next two weeks, I will partner with the King in natural and supernatural ways to demonstrate His mercy and justice in my town/city.
- ☐ Short-range goal: ____________________
- ☐ Long-range goal: ____________________

OTHER

- ☐ ____________________
- ☐ ____________________

NOTES

H

H

POWERFUL PEOPLE TAKE FULL RESPONSIBILITY FOR THE QUALITY OF LIFE THEY ARE CREATING AND THEREFORE LIVING IN.

DANNY SILK

FREE AND
RESPONSIBLE

FREE AND RESPONSIBLE

DEFINING THE CORE VALUE

Christ died to set us free from sin, death, fear, and shame in order to establish us in freedom so we can live and love as God's glorious children.
Romans 8:1–2, 15–21; Galatians 5:1; Romans 6:4, 14–22; 2 Corinthians 3:17, 5:17; 1 John 4:17–18; Luke 19:1–10

Freedom is very personal, but it is not self-centered. We have been given freedom so we may present ourselves to the Lord as a willing sacrifice, surrendered and ready to serve.
Galatians 5:13–14; Romans 12:1–2, 14:7–9, 15:1–7; Matthew 4:1–11

Freedom and responsibility are inseparable. We experience true freedom as we cooperate with the Holy Spirit to produce the fruit of self-control and use our freedom to bless others.
Galatians 5:13–25; 1 Corinthians 9:19; 2 Peter 1:5–9; 1 Corinthians 8:9–13; 1 Peter 1:13–16; John 13:12–17

We are responsible for partnering with the Holy Spirit to continually develop the foundation of our character so our character can support our growing influence and anointing.
2 Peter 1:5–9; Titus 2:11–12; Ephesians 4:1; Colossians 1:10; 1 Corinthians 6:18–20; Luke 9:54–56

WHAT DOES THIS MEAN?

Environments of freedom, responsibility, and empowerment enable people to live holy, healthy, bold, creative lives.
2 Corinthians 3:7–18; Luke 10:1–2, 17–20; Acts 2:42–47; 1 John 4:17–18; Galatians 3:23–29

Freedom is very valuable to God. He demonstrated this when He placed a sinful choice in the garden of Eden. Therefore, it is not our goal to remove sinful choices from people, but instead call them to freely love God and choose His righteousness.
Genesis 2:15–17; 2 Corinthians 3:16–17; John 14:15; Romans 12:1; 2 Peter 3:9

Usually our dreams are too small. God has big purposes for us to extend His Kingdom. As we submit our lives to Him and become excited about seeing His dreams fulfilled, we are free to dream big dreams for our lives with Him.
Ephesians 3:20; Psalm 37:4–5; Isaiah 55:1–13; 1 Corinthians 2:9–10; John 14:12–14; Matthew 6:10, 33; Genesis 12:1–3; 2 Chronicles 6:5–8

The Holy Spirit internally motivates us towards freedom, purity, and integrity.
Galatians 5:16–26; Philippians 2:13; Romans 8:14

In our freedom, if we sin or make mistakes, we must take responsibility for our actions, repent and reconcile with those affected.
Matthew 5:23–24; Hebrews 4:15–16; 1 John 1:6–10; James 5:1; Luke 19:1–10

When we are tempted to compromise our character and sin, we overcome by drawing from the power of the Holy Spirit and from our true identities as sons and daughters of God.
Romans 8:5–17; 1 John 4:4; Galatians 5:19–25; 1 Corinthians 10:13

We have God-given needs, and we honor Him when we meet these needs in ways consistent with His heart or when we freely and sacrificially lay them down, by His grace.
Philippians 4:19; 1 Corinthians 6:12–13; Ephesians 5:28–29; 1 Corinthians 7:1–7, 9:4–15; Philippians 2:5–8, 17; Romans 12:1–2

F

DO NOT MISUNDERSTAND

Freedom is not free—it cost God the death of His son. This truth motivates us to protect and value our freedom for the precious gift that it is.
Galatians 5:1; John 3:16; 1 Peter 1:18–19; Luke 4:16–21; 1 Corinthians 6:19–20

As God's children, servants, and friends, we are not free to do whatever we want; rather, we moderate our freedom to protect our connection with Him and with one another.
Galatians 5:13–14; Romans 14:13–23; Philippians 3:8; 1 Corinthians 6:19–20; Ephesians 4:1–3; 1 Corinthians 10:23–24

In our freedom, we still live a life that is submitted to the Lord.
1 Peter 2:13–17; Romans 12:1; James 4:7; Philippians 2:2–7

Perseverance is absolutely necessary to see dreams fulfilled.
Galatians 6:9; Hebrews 10:36; Philippians 3:14; James 1:12; Romans 5:1–5; Hebrews 12:1–3

Life is not about us getting everything we want. Instead, we use our freedom to love.
1 Corinthians 10:23–24; Matthew 26:39; John 15:13; 1 Corinthians 9:19

We are called to serve others and, in doing so, sometimes have to do things we do not feel like doing.
1 Peter 2:16–20; Romans 14:19–23; 1 Corinthians 13:4–7; Luke 21:16–19, 22:42; Hebrews 11:8–12

Write two of your own "What Does This Mean?" statements for *Free and Responsible*, along with one or two supporting Scriptures.

-

-

Try to think of one or two other ways the core value *Free and Responsible* could potentially be misunderstood, along with one or two Scriptures to correct these misunderstandings.

-

-

F

WHAT IS GOD SAYING TO ME?

As you read each of the four core value definitions and supporting scriptures below, take time to wait quietly with the Lord, asking Him, *"What are You saying to me about this core value?"* Use the space below each definition to journal what comes to your mind and spirit as you listen: thoughts, impressions, Scriptures, pictures, etc...

Christ died to set us free from sin, death, fear, and shame in order to establish us in freedom so we can live and love as God's glorious children.
Romans 8:15–21; Galatians 5:1; Romans 6:4, 14–22; 2 Corinthians 3:17; 2 Corinthians 5:17; 1 John 4:17–18; Luke 19:1–10

"Therefore there is now no condemnation for those who are in Christ Jesus. For the law of the Spirit of life in Christ Jesus has set you free from the law of sin and of death." - Romans 8:1–2

"It was for freedom that Christ set us free; therefore keep standing firm and do not be subject again to a yoke of slavery." - Galatians 5:1

Freedom is very personal, but it is not self-centered. We have been given freedom so we may present ourselves to the Lord as a willing sacrifice, surrendered and ready to serve.
Romans 14:7–9, 15:1–7; Matthew 4:1–11

"For you were called to freedom, brethren; only do not turn your freedom into an opportunity for the flesh, but through love serve one another. For the whole Law is fulfilled in one word, in the statement, 'You shall love your neighbor as yourself.'" - Galatians 5:13–14

"Therefore I urge you, brethren, by the mercies of God, to present your bodies a living and holy sacrifice, acceptable to God, which is your spiritual service of worship. And do not be conformed to this world, but be transformed by the renewing of your mind, so that you may prove what the will of God is, that which is good and acceptable and perfect." - Romans 12:1–2

Freedom and responsibility are inseparable. We experience true freedom as we cooperate with the Holy Spirit to produce the fruit of self-control and use our freedom to bless others.
Galatians 5:13–25; 1 Corinthians 8:9–13; 1 Peter 1:13–16; John 13:12–17

"For though I am free from all men, I have made myself a slave to all, so that I may win more."
- 1 Corinthians 9:19

"Now for this very reason also, applying all diligence, in your faith supply moral excellence, and in your moral excellence, knowledge, and in your knowledge, self-control, and in your self-control, perseverance, and in your perseverance, godliness, and in your godliness, brotherly kindness, and in your brotherly kindness, love. For if these qualities are yours and are increasing, they render you neither useless nor unfruitful in the true knowledge of our Lord Jesus Christ. For he who lacks these qualities is blind or short-sighted, having forgotten his purification from his former sins."
- 2 Peter 1:5–9

We are responsible for partnering with the Holy Spirit to continually develop the foundation of our character so our character can support our growing influence and anointing.
2 Peter 1:5–9; Colossians 1:10; 1 Corinthians 6:18–20; Luke 9:54–56

"For the grace of God has appeared, bringing salvation to all men, instructing us to deny ungodliness and worldly desires and to live sensibly, righteously and godly in the present age."
- Titus 2:11–12

"Therefore I, the prisoner of the Lord, implore you to walk in a manner worthy of the calling with which you have been called." - Ephesians 4:1

F

ACTIVATIONS

Christ died to set us free from sin, death, fear and shame, and establish us in freedom so we can live and love as God's glorious children! List three areas in your life where you are living freely and responsibly and reflect on how God brought you into this freedom.

Turn on peaceful music, quiet your mind, and ask Jesus to show you if there are any areas in your life where you are motivated by fear or circumstances instead of the Holy Spirit. For example, waiting for people to talk to you instead of being the one to take initiative to make conversation, or making decisions in order to avoid rejection from friends, family members, or coworkers. Ask God to give you a picture in your imagination of what your day will look like when you're internally motivated by the Holy Spirit and living completely free and responsible in these areas. In the space below, draw or describe whatever He shows you and then write down four words to describe how you will feel when you are living in 100% freedom.

TESTIMONIES

"I remember listening to one of our pastors explain Matthew 7:14 about the small gate and narrow way that leads to life. He said something I had never heard before. He said, 'After you get through the gate, it's like a superhighway of freedom.' It was profound to me. You mean there is freedom in Jesus? For years I thought success in my relationship with the Lord was dependent upon what I didn't do. I was a scared Christian. My only motivation was external. I didn't know I could make choices, I didn't know how to make choices. After that teaching, I began to understand that in the Kingdom there is more freedom than I could ever imagine. God isn't controlling or demanding. His love is limitless. Jesus died to make me free, but with freedom comes responsibility. I realized it is my responsibility to steward the freedom He gives me. No longer was my life about what I didn't do, but it was about what I could do. As God taught me about my freedom, I began to grow in self-control. I found myself wanting to do what was best for my relationship with Him, not just do what I felt like I wanted to do in the moment. When I live in freedom I may not always get what I want, but as I choose what will connect me to the Father, I get more than I ever thought possible."

-GABE V.

Write one story of a time when you saw His Kingdom advancing in your life or the life of someone you know.

F

MY MESSAGE

Whether teaching at your home group or falling into conversation with friends at a birthday party, use this sermon preparation guide to organize your thoughts so you can help others understand that we are free and responsible.

My favorite scriptures for this core value:

My interpretation of these scriptures:

Key points I want to communicate:

The key phrase of the testimony I'll share as an example of this core value:

Example of how these truths could be applied to a real-life situation:

The change, inspiration, impartation, and/or call to action I want others to embrace after learning we are free and responsible:

HOW AM I DOING?

Take a few minutes to reread the core value definitions at the beginning of this chapter and then rate yourself from 1–5 in each area below to help you identify strengths and opportunities for growth. Use this information to help you create personal growth goals on the following page.

1 / NEVER **2** / RARELY **3** / SOMETIMES **4** / OFTEN **5** / ALWAYS

I KNOW I AM FREE AND RESPONSIBLE

____ I can articulate it.

____ I can identify it in Scripture, books, movies, testimonies, sermons, and life.

____ I have experienced it in personal and/or corporate settings.

I DO THIS CORE VALUE

____ I am taking risks and sharing testimonies as I practice this core value.

____ I invite people into my life who exhibit, call out, and give me feedback in this value.

I BELIEVE I AM FREE AND RESPONSIBLE

____ I have identified and replaced opposing beliefs and behaviors that hinder my growth in this area.

____ I believe it even when I am alone and no one is watching.

____ My level of hope and expectation has increased in this area.

I REPRODUCE THIS CORE VALUE

____ I have it as a priority in my life.

____ I am intentionally reproducing it in others and can see their progress.

____ I have stories of how others have recognized and been impacted by it in my life.

I AM FREE AND RESPONSIBLE

____ I have consistently lived each of the prior stages for many years in a variety of settings.

____ I am an innovator, explorer, and articulator of it and people seek my wisdom concerning it.

____ I naturally multiply it. I can identify people whom I have taught and are now effectively teaching others to live this core value.

GROWING IN THIS CORE VALUE

Using your personal assessment from the previous page, ask Holy Spirit to help you write a short-term and long-term goal for each of the following areas. Remember to make your goals time-specific, measurable, and realistic. Choose one to focus on this week and, as you accomplish it, come back and check it off so you can see your growth. Below are some examples to get you started.

MYSELF

- [ ] Within the next two days, I'll set aside personal time with the Lord to present myself anew to the Him as a willing sacrifice, surrendered and ready to serve wherever and however He leads me.
- [ ] Short-range goal: ______
- [ ] Long-range goal: ______

MY HOME/FAMILY

- [ ] This week I'll begin a conversation with my family/housemates about practical ways we can create an environment of freedom, responsibility, and empowerment in our home to enable each other to live holy, healthy, bold, creative lives.
- [ ] Short-range goal: ______
- [ ] Long-range goal: ______

MY PLACE OF WORK/SCHOOL

- [ ] This week I'll grow in being free and responsible by planning my time so I arrive five minutes early to all my appointments and meetings.
- [ ] Short-range goal: ______
- [ ] Long-range goal: ______

OTHER

- [ ] ______

NOTES

WE CELEBRATE

A PERSON FOR WHO

THEY ARE WITHOUT

STUMBLING OVER

WHO THEY ARE NOT.

BILL JOHNSON

HONOR
AFFIRMS
VALUE

HONOR AFFIRMS VALUE

DEFINING THE CORE VALUE

Honor recognizes and affirms that every person is valuable and powerful. We are made in God's image; He died to restore us to relationship with Him, therefore we are significant.

Genesis 1:26–28; Ephesians 4:23–24; Psalm 139:13–16; Romans 12:10; 1 Corinthians 12:14–26; 1 Peter 2:17; Matthew 26:6–13

Honor recognizes and celebrates the best in people, in spite of our differences. We respond to people based on their God-given identity and the honor in our hearts, not their behavior or self-definition.

1 Corinthians 12:14–26; 2 Corinthians 5:16–17; James 2:1–5; Philippians 2:3; 1 Samuel 24:1–10

Honor is demonstrated through consistent respect in word and action toward those we lead, follow, love, and disagree with. While honor avoids controlling others, it also lovingly confronts, limits, and disciplines when necessary.

1 Corinthians 13:1–7; Leviticus 19:15–18; Galatians 6:1–2; Ephesians 4:14–15; Romans 2:4; Matthew 18:15; Hebrews 12:11–14; 2 Timothy 3:16–17; Luke 3:10–14

The level of honor we have for a person directly affects our ability to receive from them.

Matthew 10:40–42; Philippians 2:1–4; 1 Corinthians 4:14–20; 2 Kings 4:8–37

WHAT DOES THIS MEAN?

We love people even if we do not receive anything from them in return.
Romans 5:8; Matthew 5:43–48, 25:40, 45; Proverbs 14:31

We regularly ask God to help us see the people in our lives as He does and to encourage them with the truths He tells us about them.
2 Corinthians 5:16–17; 1 Corinthians 14:3–5; Matthew 16:17–19; Judges 6:12–16; Ephesians 1:18

We recognize where other people fit in the body of Christ, celebrate their individuality, and make room for their gifts to be expressed.
1 Corinthians 12:4–31, 14:26; Romans 12:3–5; Ephesians 4:7–16; Matthew 10:41

We love our enemies and pray for those who persecute us.
Matthew 5:43–48; Luke 9:54–56, 23:34

We honor the future generations and desire to see them prosper and do greater things than we have done.
John 14:12; Deuteronomy 31:14, 23; 2 Kings 2:9–14; 1 Chronicles 22:5–11; Acts 2:38–39

Some people need to belong before they believe. Rather than judge people outside the church, we love, serve, and speak life to them, hoping that they will soon embrace the truth of Father's love.
John 3:1-17; Romans 2:4; Mark 2:13–17; 1 Corinthians 5:5–13; Matthew 10:8; 7:50–51, 19:39–40

It is a mistake to give honor to those in leadership but not to those in our everyday lives.
1 Corinthians 12:24–26; Philippians 2:3–7; Ephesians 4:2–4; Matthew 25:40

If our brothers or sisters sin, we help them to find the root cause of their behavior so that they can be restored to wholeness.
Galatians 6:1–2; James 5:19–20; Matthew 18:15–16; Luke 17:3–4; 1 Corinthians 4:14

DO NOT MISUNDERSTAND

When necessary, we confront our brothers and sisters and call them to live up to their true identity.
1 Corinthians 4:14; Luke 9:54–56; Matthew 16:23; Titus 3:8–11; 2 Thessalonians 3:14–15

Though all are equally loved by God, we are not equally empowered by God or the community. Within God's design of authority, there are different levels of favor and position. The body of Christ is most effective when we embrace this truth while maintaining mutual honor for one another.
1 Timothy 5:17–19; 1 Corinthians 12:18, 24–28; Ephesians 4:7–16; 1 Thessalonians 5:12–13

Those in leadership should not use their authority to be destructive, manipulative, or controlling.
Matthew 25:25–28; 1 Peter 5:1–3; 1 Timothy 6:3–14; 3 John 9–11; 1 Corinthians 3:12–13

We honor others in every situation, not just when and where it's convenient.
Romans 13:7–8; 1 Peter 2:17–20, 3:8–9; John 13:34–35, 4:5–42; Matthew 19:13–15

We do not always have to agree with everyone or have the same opinions.
Ephesians 4:1–4; Romans 14:1–23; Acts 15:30–35; 2 Timothy 4:11

People can choose to behave their way out of relationship and connection with us.
Titus 3:9–11; 2 John 1:1; 2 Thessalonians 3:14–15; 1 Corinthians 5:4–6; 1 Thessalonians 5:14

Write two of your own "What Does This Mean?" statements for *Honor Affirms Value*, along with one or two supporting scriptures.

-

-

Try to think of one or two other ways the core value *Honor Affirms Value* could potentially be misunderstood, along with one or two Scriptures to correct these misunderstandings.

-

-

H

WHAT IS GOD SAYING TO ME?

As you read each of the four core value definitions and supporting scriptures below, take time to wait quietly with the Lord, asking Him, *"What are You saying to me about this core value?"* Use the space below each definition to journal what comes to your mind and spirit as you listen: thoughts, impressions, Scriptures, pictures, etc...

Honor recognizes and affirms that every person is valuable and powerful. We are made in God's image; He died to restore us to relationship with Him, therefore we are significant.
Ephesians 4:23–24; Psalm 139:13–16; Romans 12:10; 1 Corinthians 12:14–26; 1 Peter 2:17; Matthew 26:6–13

"Then God said, 'Let Us make man in Our image, according to Our likeness; and let them rule over the fish of the sea and over the birds of the sky and over the cattle and over all the earth, and over every creeping thing that creeps on the earth.' God created man in His own image, in the image of God He created him; male and female He created them. God blessed them; and God said to them, 'Be fruitful and multiply, and fill the earth, and subdue it; and rule over the fish of the sea and over the birds of the sky and over every living thing that moves on the earth.'" - Genesis 1:26–28

Honor recognizes and celebrates the best in people, in spite of our differences. We respond to people based on their God-given identity and the honor in our hearts, not their behavior or self-definition.
1 Corinthians 12:14–26; James 2:1–5; Philippians 2:3; 1 Samuel 24:1–10

"Therefore from now on we recognize no one according to the flesh; even though we have known Christ according to the flesh, yet now we know Him in this way no longer. Therefore if anyone is in Christ, he is a new creature; the old things passed away; behold, new things have come."
- 2 Corinthians 5:16–17

Honor is demonstrated through consistent respect in word and action toward those we lead, follow, love, and disagree with. While honor avoids controlling others, it also lovingly confronts, limits, and disciplines when necessary.
Leviticus 19:15–18; Galatians 6:1–2; Ephesians 4:14–15; Romans 2:4; Matthew 18:15; Hebrews 12:11–14; 2 Timothy 3:16–17; Luke 3:10–14

"If I speak with the tongues of men and of angels, but do not have love, I have become a noisy gong or a clanging cymbal. If I have the gift of prophecy, and know all mysteries and all knowledge; and if I have all faith, so as to remove mountains, but do not have love, I am nothing. And if I give all my possessions to feed the poor, and if I surrender my body to be burned, but do not have love, it profits me nothing. Love is patient, love is kind and is not jealous; love does not brag and is not arrogant, does not act unbecomingly; it does not seek its own, is not provoked, does not take into account a wrong suffered, does not rejoice in unrighteousness, but rejoices with the truth; bears all things, believes all things, hopes all things, endures all things." - 1 Corinthians 13:1–7

The level of honor we have for a person directly affects our ability to receive from them.
Philippians 2:1–4; 1 Corinthians 4:14–20; 2 Kings 4:8–37

"He who receives you receives Me, and he who receives Me receives Him who sent Me. He who receives a prophet in the name of a prophet shall receive a prophet's reward; and he who receives a righteous man in the name of a righteous man shall receive a righteous man's reward. And whoever in the name of a disciple gives to one of these little ones even a cup of cold water to drink, truly I say to you, he shall not lose his reward." - Matthew 10:40–42

H

ACTIVATIONS

Ask the Holy Spirit to bring to mind someone who has hurt you or someone you're challenged to love and/or like. Wait silently for a few moments and ask God to give you His love for that person. Then ask the Lord to give you His perspective of how He sees the person. Journal whatever He shows you and ask Him to give you ideas of how you can bless and honor that person this week.

Ask the Lord to show you a close family member or friend you can honor with a creative, random act of kindness. Dream with God to come up with an idea uniquely designed to show love and value to that person, such as cooking a special meal, giving a unique gift, or sending him or her a prophetic word.

Increase your honor and thankfulness for people around you who are working hard to serve others, but usually go unnoticed. When you see these people, thank them for their hard work. If you see someone doing his or her job really well, ask to speak to their manager and tell them what an excellent job the person is doing.

TESTIMONIES

"When I came to BSSM I was in my mid 30s and had spent seven years in full-time ministry. While I certainly didn't feel like I knew it all, when I was paired with a mentor who was barely 20 years old, I didn't have a great deal of expectation to receive much from her. One day during worship, early in the school year, I made a conscious decision to put my whole heart behind honoring her as my mentor. I knew no matter how old she was or what life experience she had, there would be things I would glean from her. The very next day, during a meeting with her, I had one of my most significant encounters with the Lord and He broke off a fear of rejection I had battled almost my whole life. As I continued to honor her as my mentor, she had a huge influence on my life throughout my school year and continues to inspire me to this day."

-KATRINA S.

Write two stories of times you saw honor affirm the value of someone and how this impacted their life.

-

-

H

MY MESSAGE

Whether teaching kids at summer camp or talking to a stranger on the bus, use this sermon preparation guide to organize your thoughts so you can help others understand that honor affirms value.

My favorite scriptures for this core value:

My interpretation of these scriptures:

Key points I want to communicate:

The key phrase of the testimony I'll share as an example of this core value:

Example of how these truths could be applied to a real-life situation:

The change, inspiration, impartation, and/or call to action I want others to embrace after learning that honor affirms value:

HOW AM I DOING?

Take a few minutes to reread the core value definitions at the beginning of this chapter and then rate yourself from 1–5 in each area below to help you identify strengths and opportunities for growth. Use this information to help you create personal growth goals on the following page.

1 / NEVER **2** / RARELY **3** / SOMETIMES **4** / OFTEN **5** / ALWAYS

I KNOW HONOR AFFIRMS VALUE

____ I can identify it in Scripture, books, movies, testimonies, sermons, and life.

____ I have experienced it in personal and/or corporate settings.

____ I have a growing affection for it and I desire to apply it.

I DO THIS CORE VALUE

____ I am taking risks and sharing testimonies as I practice this core value.

____ I invite people into my life who exhibit, call out, and give me feedback in this value.

I BELIEVE HONOR AFFIRMS VALUE

____ I have identified and replaced opposing beliefs and behaviors that hinder my growth in this area.

____ I believe it even when I am alone and no one is watching.

____ I usually view and respond to life through the lens of it.

I REPRODUCE HONOR AFFIRMS VALUE

____ I bring the strength of it as I serve others and build community.

____ I am intentionally reproducing it in others and can see their progress.

____ I have stories of how others have recognized and been impacted by it in my life.

I AM THIS CORE VALUE

____ I have consistently lived each of the prior stages for many years in a variety of settings.

____ It is my natural response as I make decisions and respond to situations in my everyday life.

____ I understand the spiritual authority I have in this area and intentionally influence those around me.

GROWING IN THIS CORE VALUE

Using your personal assessment from the previous page, ask Holy Spirit to help you write a short-term and long-term goal for each of the following areas. Remember to make your goals time-specific, measurable, and realistic. Choose one to focus on this week and, as you accomplish it, come back and check it off so you can see your growth. Below are some examples to get you started.

MYSELF

- ☐ For the next 48 hours, I will intentionally honor people by speaking out loud the nice things I notice about them. For example: *I like your hair today; I find it easy to listen to you; I love how passionate that person is.*
- ☐ Short-range goal: ____________________
- ☐ Long-range goal: ____________________

MY HOME/FAMILY

- ☐ Within the next three days, I'll ask the people with whom I'm close to tell me one way I can improve in honoring them and then look for ways to honor them in that way.
- ☐ Short-range goal: ____________________
- ☐ Long-range goal: ____________________

MY PLACE OF WORK/SCHOOL

- ☐ This week, I will look for opportunities to verbally honor and value my local and national leaders I disagree with, both when I'm talking about them and praying for them.
- ☐ Short-range goal: ____________________
- ☐ Long-range goal: ____________________

OTHER

- ☐ ____________________
- ☐ ____________________

NOTES

H

H

IT IS BEYOND
THE REALM OF
POSSIBILITIES THAT
ONE HAS THE ABILITY
TO OUTGIVE GOD.

CHARLES SPURGEON

GENEROUS
LIKE MY
FATHER

GENEROUS LIKE MY FATHER

DEFINING THE CORE VALUE

God is extravagantly generous and our generosity is a response and reflection of Him. He is a good Father who gives good gifts to His children.
James 1:17; Psalm 103:1–5; John 3:16; Ephesians 1:3; 2 Corinthians 8:9, 9:8; Acts 14:17; Matthew 7:7–11; Luke 15:11–32

The thread of God's generosity weaves through His creation, covenants, Israel's economics, the gospel and the Kingdom as He consistently models that it is more blessed to give than to receive.
Psalm 65:9–13; Deuteronomy 28:1–14, 7:9; 2 Corinthians 8:9; Matthew 20:28; Ephesians 1:3, 7–8; James 1:5; Acts 20:35; Mark 12:41–43

God has blessed us in every way so that we can be generous in every way to advance the gospel. Joyfully giving our time, affection, talents and money, attracts God's attention, draws heaven's blessing, produces transformation, and enables Him to trust us with the true riches of the Kingdom.
2 Corinthians 9:6–15; Acts 10:3–6; Malachi 3:10–12; Deuteronomy 8:18; Acts 2:43–47; Matthew 10:7–8; Luke 16:10–13; Acts 4:32–37

Generosity confronts our poverty mentality, changing the way we interact with the world. No longer anxious because we mistakenly believe provision is scarce, we are confident that God multiplies resources and is eager to rescue and prosper people.
2 Corinthians 9:6–15; Philippians 4:19; Ephesians 3:20–21; 1 King 17:10–16; 2 Kings 4:1–7; 3 John 2; Matthew 6:25–34; Jeremiah 29:11; Deuteronomy 28:11–13; Exodus 3:8; Matthew 14:13–21

Generosity releases joy, blessing, and favor into our lives. As we give, it will be given to us, pressed down, shaken together, and running over!
Luke 6:38; Isaiah 58:6–12; Proverbs 11:25; Acts 2:43–47; Philippians 4:17–19; 1 Timothy 6:17–19; Luke 18:29–30, 19:1–10

WHAT DOES THIS MEAN?

Generosity is an expression of our trust in God's provision—a declaration that our treasure is truly in heaven. As I take care of His priorities, He will look after mine.
1 Timothy 6:17–19; Philippians 4:18–19; Acts 4:33–37; Matthew 6:19–33; 2 Corinthians 9:8–12; Genesis 13:5–18

Generosity is a mindset. The poorest person on earth can live generously. Even if we don't have many resources, we always have something to give.
Luke 21:1–4; Mark 6:30–44; 2 Corinthians 8:13–15; Matthew 10:42; Acts 3:1–9

We do not only give out of our abundance or convenience. Sacrifice is vital to a lifestyle of generosity. The Lord notices when our giving is costly to us.
Luke 21:1–4; 2 Corinthians 8:1–4; Luke 6:30–36, 10:30–37; 2 Samuel 24:24–25; Romans 8:32; Mark 9:41

Generosity should permeate our marriages, families, businesses, and communities, and benefit generations yet to come.
Ephesians 5:25; James 1:19; Proverbs 31:16–19; Mark 7:9–13; 2 Corinthians 8:14; 1 Timothy 5:4; John 3:16–18; Leviticus 19:9–10; Proverbs 13:22

God promised Israel a "land flowing with milk and honey." Though we do not give just to receive, God is a rewarder and wants to bless materially as well as spiritually, emotionally, and physically.
Exodus 3:8; Luke 6:38; Hebrews 11:6; 3 John 2; 2 Corinthians 9:7–8; Psalm 103:1–5; Proverbs 11:24–25

As seen throughout history, generosity is essential for the healing and development of the nations. God is attracted to generosity in believers and unbelievers alike.
Isaiah 58:6–12; 1 Chronicles 29:1–9; Acts 10:1–4; Exodus 35:22–36:5; Nehemiah 2:1–8, 5:14–19; Ezra 1:1–11; Matthew 5:44; Proverbs 25:21

Generosity creates unity.
Acts 4:32–37; 2 Corinthians 8:14; 1 John 3:16–18; Philippians 4:10–19; 2 Corinthians 9:12–15

WHAT DOES THIS MEAN? (CONTINUED)

Generosity causes people to be thankful and is an opportunity for others to encounter the Lord's goodness.
2 Corinthians 9:10–13; Romans 2:4; 2 Kings 6:22–23; Luke 9:12–17; Philippians 4:15–16; Matthew 5:16

The Lord celebrates generosity to the poor and to fellow Christians as a gift to Himself. A generous heart cares for the widow and orphan, the marginalized and hurting.
Proverbs 14:31, 19:17; James 1:27; Psalm 68:5–6; Luke 19:1–10; Galatians 2:10; Mark 9:41; Matthew 25:34–40; Deuteronomy 15:12–14

DO NOT MISUNDERSTAND

Being poor, middle-class or rich is neither a virtue nor a sin. Christians should cooperate with the Holy Spirit according to their situation, assignment, season of life, and/or calling. Some might be in poverty, needing the Kingdom's generous breakthrough just to survive; some may live simply, needing and creating little wealth, yet still thriving; while others may create and steward wealth to live and give generously and foster society, establishing the poor, creating work and abundance, producing a legacy that benefits themselves, society, and the Kingdom.
2 Corinthians 8:9; Philippians 4:11–13; Luke 9:58; Acts 4:36; Matthew 27:57–60; Acts 20:32–36; 1 Corinthians 4:8–17; Acts 16:14–15; Job 29; Genesis 24:35, 26:12–14; 2 Chronicles 32:26–28; Proverbs 3:9–10, 10:22, 22:3–4; 2 Timothy 6:17–19

Money is not evil but the love of money is a root of all kinds of evil. So we do not love it but rather use it to build His Kingdom. Money is a tool, and in human hands it can be a blessing or a curse. It should never be our master, but it is a powerful servant.
1 Timothy 6:9–10; Matthew 6:19–24; Deuteronomy 8:18; Malachi 3:10–12; Luke 16:8–15

The motivation for our giving is more important than what we give. We don't give out of a sense of guilt or manipulation, nor to impress or control God or people.
1 Samuel 15:19–23; 2 Corinthians 9:7; 1 Corinthians 13:3; Matthew 6:1–4; 1 John 3:17–18;

DO NOT MISUNDERSTAND (CONTINUED)

Acts 5:1–5, 8:18–24

As always, we carefully follow the Holy Spirit's voice while learning generosity. We do not give impulsively, but rather ask the Father what He thinks about each situation.

John 5:19, 16:13; Matthew 19:16–22; 1 Timothy 6:17–19; Acts 5:1–5; 1 Samuel 15:19–23

Our generosity should not be at the expense of others. Being generous while consistently not repaying debt or paying bills is not true generosity, but rather presumption, as we are giving away the money promised to another.

Mark 7:9–13, 12:17; 1 Timothy 5:4; Romans 13:7

Generosity is often expressed in secret, though it doesn't have to be in order to bring glory to God.

Matthew 6:2–4; 2 Corinthians 8:24, 9:10–15; Acts 4:32–37; 1 Chronicles 29:1–9; Exodus 35:22

Generosity is a form of honor that we can extend to both the poor and the wealthy.

John 12:1–8; 1 Kings 10:10; Genesis 14:17–20; Luke 23:50-56

G

Write two of your own "What Does This Mean?" statements for *Generous like my Father,* along with one or two supporting Scriptures.

-

-

Try to think of one or two other ways the core value *Generous like my Father* could potentially be misunderstood, along with one or two Scriptures to correct these misunderstandings.

-

-

WHAT IS GOD SAYING TO ME?

As you read each of the five core value definitions and supporting scriptures below, take time to wait quietly with the Lord, asking Him, *"What are You saying to me about this core value?"* Use the space below each definition to journal what comes to your mind and spirit as you listen: thoughts, impressions, Scriptures, pictures, etc...

God is extravagantly generous and our generosity is a response and reflection of Him. He is a good Father who gives good gifts to His children.
James 1:17; Psalm 103:1–5; John 3:16; Ephesians 1:3; 2 Corinthians 8:9, 9:8; Acts 14:17; Matthew 7:7–11; Luke 15:11–32

"Every good thing given and every perfect gift is from above, coming down from the Father of lights, with whom there is no variation or shifting shadow." - James 1:17

"Bless the Lord, O my soul, And all that is within me, bless His holy name. Bless the Lord, O my soul, And forget none of His benefits; Who pardons all your iniquities, Who heals all your diseases; Who redeems your life from the pit, Who crowns you with lovingkindness and compassion; Who satisfies your years with good things, So that your youth is renewed like the eagle." - Psalm 103:1–5

The thread of God's generosity weaves through His creation, covenants, Israel's economics, the gospel and the Kingdom as He consistently models that it is more blessed to give than to receive.
Deuteronomy 28:1–14, 7:9; 2 Corinthians 8:9; Matthew 20:28; Ephesians 1:3, 7–8; James 1:5; Acts 20:35; Mark 12:41–43

"You visit the earth and cause it to overflow; You greatly enrich it; The stream of God is full of water; You prepare their grain, for thus You prepare the earth. You water its furrows abundantly, You settle its ridges, You soften it with showers, You bless its growth. You have crowned the year with Your bounty, And Your paths drip with fatness. The pastures of the wilderness drip, And the hills gird themselves with rejoicing. The meadows are clothed with flocks, And the valleys are covered with grain; They shout for joy, yes, they sing." - Psalm 65:9–13

G

God has blessed us in every way so that we can be generous in every way to advance the gospel. Joyfully giving our time, affection, talents and money, attracts God's attention, draws heaven's blessing, produces transformation, and enables Him to trust us with the true riches of the Kingdom.

2 Corinthians 9:6–15; Malachi 3:10–12; Deuteronomy 8:18; Acts 2:43–47; Matthew 10:7–8; Luke 16:10–13; Acts 4:32–37

"About the ninth hour of the day he clearly saw in a vision an angel of God who had just come in and said to him, 'Cornelius!' And fixing his gaze on him and being much alarmed, he said, 'What is it, Lord?' And he said to him, 'Your prayers and alms have ascended as a memorial before God. Now dispatch some men to Joppa and send for a man named Simon, who is also called Peter; he is staying with a tanner named Simon, whose house is by the sea.'" - Acts 10:3–6

Generosity confronts our poverty mentality, changing the way we interact with the world. No longer anxious because we mistakenly believe provision is scarce, we are confident that God multiplies resources and is eager to rescue and prosper people.

2 Corinthians 9:6–15; 1 King 17:10–16; 2 Kings 4:1–7; 3 John 2; Matthew 6:25–34; Jeremiah 29:11; Deuteronomy 28:11–13; Exodus 3:8; Matthew 14:13–21

"And my God will supply all your needs according to His riches in glory in Christ Jesus."
- Philippians 4:19

"Now to Him who is able to do far more abundantly beyond all that we ask or think, according to the power that works within us, to Him be the glory in the church and in Christ Jesus to all generations forever and ever. Amen." - Ephesians 3:20–21

Generosity releases joy, blessing, and favor into our lives. As we give, it will be given to us, pressed down, shaken together, and running over!
Isaiah 58:6–12; Acts 2:43–47; Philippians 4:17–19; 1 Timothy 6:17–19; Luke 18:29–30, 19:1–10

"Give, and it will be given to you. They will pour into your lap a good measure—pressed down, shaken together, and running over. For by your standard of measure it will be measured to you in return." - Luke 6:38

"The generous man will be prosperous, and he who waters will himself be watered."
- Proverbs 11:25

G

ACTIVATIONS

Radical generosity is one of the keys to living in revival and abundance. God is extravagantly generous and our generosity is a response and reflection of Him. Ask the Holy Spirit to bring to mind someone specific in your family, neighborhood, school, or workplace that He wants you to bless. Ask Him what He would like you to give that person and then boldly step out in generosity and do it! Write down the name of the person He brings to mind and what He wants you to give them.

Are there areas of your life where you have not yet seen God's abundant provision? If so, list those areas below and then ask the Holy Spirit to give you new ideas and inspiration for how you can partner with Him to see His provision in each of those areas.

How can you begin to live a life of generosity? In the space below list the talents and resources God has given you and then ask Him for creative ideas for how you could use them to bless others. Once you've made your list, share it with two friends or family members and ask them what talents and resources they have that they can use to bless others.

My Talents & Resources

How I Can Use Them To Bless Others

TESTIMONIES

"One evening, a thought came to me to contact a person I'd seen in school that day and ask him how he was doing with paying for his upcoming mission trip. He told me so far he'd only been able to pay a few dollars. After talking with him, I knew the Lord was prompting me to pay off his trip. This act of generosity was just the beginning of the fulfillment of promises God had given him concerning his mission trip. Then the Lord told me He wanted to bless me abundantly for the investment I'd made in my classmate's life, but I had no idea how He would do it. Prior to this experience, I had invested in an oil company that hadn't made money in years. However, after I paid off my classmate's trip, the company's stock began to rise and I earned $2,000: the same amount I had invested in my friend's trip! I didn't think the increase would continue, so I asked my broker to help me sell. Due to difficulties with my bank, I wasn't able to sell for another week and during that time the increase continued! When it sold I made a gain of three times what I had given! It seemed that, in His generosity, God had delayed the sale for a week so I could get the amount He wanted to give me and nothing less! It truly is impossible to outgive God!"

-LARS

Write two stories of when you, or someone you know, was generous like your Father and how lives were impacted by that generosity.

-

-

G

MY MESSAGE

Whether preaching in a prison or chatting with friends at school, use this sermon preparation guide to organize your thoughts so you can help others understand the importance of living generously.

My favorite scriptures for this core value:

My interpretation of these scriptures:

Key points I want to communicate:

The key phrase of the testimony I'll share as an example of this core value:

Example of how these truths could be applied to a real-life situation:

The change, inspiration, impartation, and/or call to action I want others to embrace after learning to live generously:

HOW AM I DOING?

Take a few minutes to reread the core value definitions at the beginning of this chapter and then rate yourself from 1–5 in each area below to help you identify strengths and opportunities for growth. Use this information to help you create personal growth goals on the following page.

1 / NEVER **2** / RARELY **3** / SOMETIMES **4** / OFTEN **5** / ALWAYS

I KNOW THIS CORE VALUE

____ I can articulate it.

____ I have experienced it in personal and/or corporate settings.

____ I have a growing affection for it and I desire to apply it.

I DO THIS CORE VALUE

____ I am taking risks and sharing testimonies as I practice this core value.

____ I invite people into my life who exhibit, call out, and give me feedback in this value.

I BELIEVE THIS CORE VALUE

____ I have identified and replaced opposing beliefs and behaviors that hinder my growth in this area.

____ My level of hope and expectation has increased in this area.

____ I usually view and respond to life through the lens of it.

I REPRODUCE THIS CORE VALUE

____ I have it as a priority in my life.

____ I bring the strength of it as I serve others and build community.

____ I have stories of how others have recognized and been impacted by it in my life.

I AM GENEROUS LIKE MY FATHER

____ I have consistently lived each of the prior stages for many years in a variety of settings.

____ It is my natural response as I make decisions and respond to situations in my everyday life.

____ I naturally multiply it. I can identify people whom I have taught and are now effectively teaching others to live this core value.

GROWING IN THIS CORE VALUE

Using your personal assessment from the previous page, ask Holy Spirit to help you write a short-term and long-term goal for each of the following areas. Remember to make your goals time-specific, measurable, and realistic. Choose one to focus on this week and, as you accomplish it, come back and check it off so you can see your growth. Below are some examples to get you started.

MYSELF

- ☐ Within the next three days, I'll spend 30 minutes identifying and replacing any opposing beliefs and/or behaviors I have that could be hindering my growth in becoming generous like my Father.
- ☐ Short-range goal: ____________________
- ☐ Long-range goal: ____________________

MY HOME/FAMILY

- ☐ This week I will ask my family members/roommates to join me in sacrificially giving of our time, energy, and/or finances to help care for widows or orphans in our community.
- ☐ Short-range goal: ____________________
- ☐ Long-range goal: ____________________

MY PLACE OF WORK/SCHOOL

- ☐ Before the end of the week, I will give two of my coworkers/classmates an opportunity to encounter the Lord's goodness by blessing them with extravagant generosity.
- ☐ Short-range goal: ____________________
- ☐ Long-range goal: ____________________

OTHER

- ☐ ____________________
- ☐ ____________________

NOTES

G

WE ARE CALLED
TO BE THE LIGHT
OF THE WORLD,
NOT THE LIGHT OF
THE CHURCH.

KRIS VALLOTTON

HOPE IN
A GLORIOUS
CHURCH

HOPE IN A GLORIOUS CHURCH

DEFINING THE CORE VALUE

The church is the bride of Christ and she will successfully fulfill His great commission to make disciples of all nations, which means the nations will experience transformation.
Ephesians 5:25–27; Matthew 28:16–20; Acts 1:8; Psalm 2:8; Revelation 11:15; Isaiah 54:3–5, 60:1–5; Acts 2

We work to leave a legacy and an inheritance for future generations, just as previous generations have done for us. While anticipating Christ's glorious return, we simply do not know when He will come, which should inspire us to have a long-term earthly vision.
Proverbs 13:22; Acts 2:39; 2 Timothy 2:1–2; Titus 2:11–14; James 5:7–8; Isaiah 9:6–7; Matthew 25:1–29; Hebrews 11:4–30

We are not looking to escape the world but to see Christ's victory manifested in individuals and nations, even in the face of resistance and conflict.
John 17:15–18; Luke 10:2–3; Matthew 28:18–19; Hebrews 12:1–3; John 16:33; Revelation 11:15; Acts 13:13–52

The church is called to overcome in all circumstances: in times of suffering and persecution, but also in times of prosperity and great influence.
John 16:33; Revelation 3:5, 21; Philippians 4:11–13; Isaiah 41:10; 1 John 4:4, 5:4; Romans 8:37–39; 1 Chronicles 28:6–10; 1 Kings 5:3–5; Acts 4:13–37

WHAT DOES THIS MEAN?

The church, both local and global, may not be glorious yet, but the Lord has promised she will be. So we love and serve our church into becoming the glorious bride she was created to be.
Ephesians 5:25–27, 4:11–16; Revelation 19:7–9; Galatians 6:1–2, 10

We are called to be the light of the world, not the light of the church.
Matthew 5:14–16; Mark 2:16–17; Isaiah 60:1–3; Jonah 4:10; Genesis 22:17–18; Matthew 28:19–20

We seek to disciple individuals, families, cities, and nations because the Kingdom of this world has become and is becoming the Kingdom of our God.
Matthew 28:18–20; Revelation 11:15; Psalm 2:8–12; Acts 14:21–28; Isaiah 61:1–11; Luke 4:18–21

We have been given responsibility and supernatural power to bring about transformation; therefore, we refuse to have a mindset that empowers the devil and disempowers the church.
Matthew 13:31–33; Isaiah 61:1–11; Luke 4:18–21; Matthew 10:8, 16:18–19; John 20:22–23; 1 John 4:4; Colossians 2:15

We remember and thank God for what He has done, knowing He is more than able to do it again.
Hebrews 13:8; 1 Chronicles 16:23–36; 2 Chronicles 20; Joshua 4:1–9; Psalm 119:2, 111; Romans 15:4; Revelation 12:11, 19:10

We serve and encourage leaders in society, whether or not they are believers, and work with them to build communities of honor, health, and wholeness.
1 Timothy 2:1–2; Romans 13:1–7; 1 Peter 2:13–17; John 13:34–35; 1 Timothy 5:17–19; Genesis 45:7–8; Job 29

We put our trust in God, not in the prosperity and power of governments.
Philippians 3:20; Jeremiah 17:5–8; Hebrews 12:28–29; Matthew 6:24–26; Psalm 20:6–7; Proverbs 23:1–3

WHAT DOES THIS MEAN? (CONTINUED)

We see every obstacle as an opportunity for Christ to bring answers.
Philippians 1:12–20; Romans 8:28–29; Genesis 50:20; Isaiah 54:17; Psalm 34:19; Deuteronomy 31:6

Prophetic words concerning leadership and government should be consistent with God's mission to seek and save the lost and should flow from a heart of love, hope and empathy, rather than wrath and judgement.
1 Corinthians 14:3; Romans 14:19; Luke 9:53–56; Romans 5:20; John 12:46–50, 3:16–17; 1 Timothy 2:4

We equip believers to live a naturally supernatural lifestyle so that they can bring transformation to their areas of influence.
Ephesians 4:11–16; Hebrews 10:24; Luke 9:1–6, 10:1–21; Ephesians 4:11–13

DO NOT MISUNDERSTAND

God is already at work in the darkest places and nations of the world.
Romans 5:20–21; Psalm 139:7–12; Jonah 1:1–2, 4:1–2, 10–11; Acts 8:26–40

The Kingdom is always expanding into new areas of influence in the world.
Isaiah 9:6–7; Daniel 7:13–14; 2 Corinthians 3:17–18; Matthew 13:31–33; Ephesians 2:10, 3:8–20; Habakkuk 2:14

We are not giving up on the world and just waiting to go to Heaven.
John 3:16–17; 2 Peter 3:9; Matthew 5:13–16, 43–45

We do not need to become like the world in order to powerfully influence it.
1 John 2:15–17; John 17:13–19, 15:19; Philippians 2:14–15; Mark 2:15–17; Matthew 11:16–19

Not everyone will be enthusiastic about the Kingdom being established. We must be prepared to experience resistance, rejection, and persecution.
2 Timothy 3:12; Matthew 5:11–12, 10:21–23; John 15:18–27; Psalm 34:18–20; Luke 21:16–19; Acts 19:23–27

Write two of your own "What Does This Mean?" statements for *Hope in a Glorious Church*, along with one or two supporting Scriptures.

-
-

Try to think of one or two other ways the core value *Hope in a Glorious Church* could potentially be misunderstood, along with one or two Scriptures to correct these misunderstandings.

-
-

H

WHAT IS GOD SAYING TO ME?

As you read each of the four core value definitions and supporting scriptures below, take time to wait quietly with the Lord, asking Him, *"What are You saying to me about this core value?"* Use the space below each definition to journal what comes to your mind and spirit as you listen: thoughts, impressions, Scriptures, pictures, etc...

The church is the bride of Christ and she will successfully fulfill His great commission to make disciples of all nations, which means the nations will experience transformation.
Acts 1:8; Matthew 28:16–20; Psalm 2:8; Revelation 11:15; Isaiah 54:3–5, 60:1–5; Acts 2

"Husbands, love your wives, just as Christ also loved the church and gave Himself up for her, so that He might sanctify her, having cleansed her by the washing of water with the word, that He might present to Himself the church in all her glory, having no spot or wrinkle or any such thing; but that she would be holy and blameless." - Ephesians 5:25–27

We work to leave a legacy and an inheritance for future generations, just as previous generations have done for us. While anticipating Christ's glorious return, we simply do not know when He will come, which should inspire us to have a long-term earthly vision.
2 Timothy 2:1–2; Titus 2:11–14; James 5:7–8; Isaiah 9:6–7; Matthew 25:1–29; Hebrews 11:4–30

"A good man leaves an inheritance to his children's children, and the wealth of the sinner is stored up for the righteous." - Proverbs 13:22

"For the promise is for you and your children and for all who are far off, as many as the Lord our God will call to Himself." - Acts 2:39

We are not looking to escape the world but to see Christ's victory manifested in individuals and nations, even in the face of resistance and conflict.
Matthew 28:18–19; Hebrews 12:1–3; John 16:33; Revelation 11:15; Acts 13:13–52

"I do not ask You to take them out of the world, but to keep them from the evil one. They are not of the world, even as I am not of the world. Sanctify them in the truth; Your word is truth. As You sent Me into the world, I also have sent them into the world." - John 17:15–18

"And He was saying to them, 'The harvest is plentiful, but the laborers are few; therefore beseech the Lord of the harvest to send out laborers into His harvest. Go; behold, I send you out as lambs in the midst of wolves.'" - Luke 10:2–3

The church is called to overcome in all circumstances: in times of suffering and persecution, but also in times of prosperity and great influence.
Revelation 3:5, 21; Philippians 4:11–13; Isaiah 41:10; 1 John 4:4, 5:4; Romans 8:37–39; 1 Chronicles 28:6–10; 1 Kings 5:3–5; Acts 4:13–37

"These things I have spoken to you, so that in Me you may have peace. In the world you have tribulation, but take courage; I have overcome the world." - John 16:33

"Not that I speak from want, for I have learned to be content in whatever circumstances I am. I know how to get along with humble means, and I also know how to live in prosperity; in any and every circumstance I have learned the secret of being filled and going hungry, both of having abundance and suffering need. I can do all things through Him who strengthens me."
- Philippians 4:11–13

H

ACTIVATIONS

Do an internet search for three ways in which the world is getting better and list them below, along with your thoughts on how they could continue to improve.

List two ways you are currently, or would like to be, building a legacy and an inheritance in your life. Invite Holy Spirit to speak to you as you imagine the outcomes He could achieve through you and other like-minded believers.

TESTIMONIES

"As the pastor of a church in Florida, I longed to see my congregation view themselves as change agents, not simply lovers of Jesus waiting for the trumpet blast to sound at the end of the world. One Sunday morning I played and danced to the song, 'Wherever We Go.' The lyrics say, 'Wherever we go the dumb get wise, the crime rates drop and the markets rise, bullies make nice, crooks repent, the ozone layer shows improvement... This is the message we spread, bringing life to the dead.' From then on I declared that we were no longer going to just defend what we believe, but we are going to infiltrate our community with all God has placed inside of us. I told them we are going to be a mission outpost that sends out special-forces missionaries into the thick of battle to win back what the enemy has stolen. Something shifted in my congregation that day. Our whole church became full of vibrant life, expectation, and joy as were realized we could love the supposedly unlovable and leak God's Presence wherever we went. We became known as the 'alive' church. Life and ministry became delightful and fulfilling!"

-PAUL K.

Write a testimony of when you've seen a group of people, city, or nation positively impacted by the legacy left by a previous generation of the church.

H

MY MESSAGE

Whether speaking to your church leadership team or talking with a person who believes God wants things to get worse and worse, use this sermon preparation guide to organize your thoughts so you can help others understand what it means to have hope in Christ's glorious church.

My favorite scriptures for this core value:

My interpretation of these scriptures:

Key points I want to communicate:

The key phrase of the testimony I'll share as an example of this core value:

Example of how these truths could be applied to a real-life situation:

The change, inspiration, impartation, and/or call to action I want others to embrace after learning how to hope in a glorious bride of Christ:

HOW AM I DOING?

Take a few minutes to reread the core value definitions at the beginning of this chapter and then rate yourself from 1–5 in each area below to help you identify strengths and opportunities for growth. Use this information to help you create personal growth goals on the following page.

1 / NEVER **2** / RARELY **3** / SOMETIMES **4** / OFTEN **5** / ALWAYS

I KNOW THIS CORE VALUE

___ I can articulate it.

___ I can identify it in Scripture, books, movies, testimonies, sermons, and life.

___ I have a growing affection for it and I desire to apply it.

I DO THIS CORE VALUE

___ I am taking risks and sharing testimonies as I practice this core value.

___ I invite people into my life who exhibit, call out, and give me feedback in this value.

I BELIEVE IN HOPE IN A GLORIOUS CHURCH

___ I have identified and replaced opposing beliefs and behaviors that hinder my growth in this area.

___ My level of hope and expectation has increased in this area.

___ I usually view and respond to life through the lens of it.

I REPRODUCE HOPE IN A GLORIOUS CHURCH

___ I have it as a priority in my life.

___ I bring the strength of it as I serve others and build community.

___ I am intentionally reproducing it in others and can see their progress.

I AM THIS CORE VALUE

___ I have consistently lived each of the prior stages for many years in a variety of settings.

___ I am an innovator, explorer, and articulator of it and people seek my wisdom concerning it.

___ I understand the spiritual authority I have in this area and intentionally influence those around me.

H

GROWING IN THIS CORE VALUE

Using your personal assessment from the previous page, ask Holy Spirit to help you write a short-term and long-term goal for each of the following areas. Remember to make your goals time-specific, measurable, and realistic. Choose one to focus on this week and, as you accomplish it, come back and check it off so you can see your growth. Below are some examples to get you started.

MYSELF

- ☐ Over the next three days, I'll look for examples of this core value in daily life, such as Scripture, books, movies, testimonies, sermons, etc. and write them down in a place where I'll find them again.
- ☐ Short-range goal:
- ☐ Long-range goal:

MY HOME/FAMILY

- ☐ This week my family/housemates and I will look for one practical way we can encourage our pastor(s) and love and serve our church into becoming the glorious bride she was created to be.
- ☐ Short-range goal:
- ☐ Long-range goal:

MY PLACE OF WORK/SCHOOL

- ☐ Within the next few days, I'll learn the names of all my local city leaders, pray for each of them twice a week for the rest of the month, and write one of them a letter of encouragement thanking them for their service.
- ☐ Short-range goal:
- ☐ Long-range goal:

OTHER

- ☐

NOTES

H

KINGDOM CULTURE DECLARATION

James 3:4 says our tongues are like a small rudder that turns a great ship. So, in some measure, we can steer our lives with our words. We read in Proverbs 18:21 that "death and life are in the power of the tongue." Applying Paul's instruction in Philippians 4:8, we intentionally think, verbalize, and practice whatever is noble, true, right, lovely, admirable, and praiseworthy.

When we speak the truth out loud it sharpens our thinking and orients our hearts. It creates a roadmap for our soul and edifies our spirit. Proclaiming truth isn't merely wishful self-talk. Rather, it interrupts the potentially negative dialogue in our heads with profound truth. Far from hype or mysticism, it's learning and routinely agreeing with what God says to be true. Making a declaration is purposeful, accurate thinking connected with faith-filled emotion to help transform us.

In faith, speak the following statement out loud over your life as a prayer that this is who you are and where you are headed. In doing so you are partnering with the Holy Spirit to see His Kingdom come on earth as it is in heaven.

At my core I believe...

God is Good
Salvation Creates Joyful Identity
I am Responsive to Grace
I am Focused on His Presence
I am Creating Healthy Family
God's Word Transforms Me
God is Still Speaking
Jesus Empowers Supernatural Ministry
His Kingdom is Advancing
I am Free and Responsible
Honor Affirms Value
I am Generous like my Father
I have Hope in a Glorious Church
At my core, I am REVIVAL!

NOTES

Core Values Create Kingdom Culture

Page 1: "be fruitful and multiply," Genesis 1:28
Page 1: "set of shared attitudes," Merriam-Webster
"Definition of Culture." Web. 22 Nov. 2016

Page 1: Sire, J. W. (2009). The Universe Next Door: A basic worldview catalog (5th ed.). Downers Grove, IL: InterVarsity Press; pg. 10

Page 3: Vallotton: "distinction between aspirational values," Kris Vallotton, www.krisvallotton.com

Page 2: "fruit of the Holy Spirit," Galatians 5:22

ABOUT THE AUTHOR

Dann Farrelly has been on staff at Bethel since 1991, working as an associate pastor and as the head of Biblical Studies and dean of Bethel School of Supernatural Ministry (BSSM). Since its inception in 1998, BSSM has grown from 36 students to well over 2,300, deploying revivalists into their own particular places of influence throughout the world.

He is a Biblical Studies graduate of Simpson University and holds a Master of Divinity from Fuller Theological Seminary. As a lifelong believer, he answered God's call to a career of ministry at the age of 17. With a pastor's heart and a love of Scripture, Dann is uniquely gifted to bring rich and practical insights from the Word of God with wit, wisdom, and anointing. He loves to see people find their true joy in the Father's deep affection for them.

He has been a catalyst to breakthrough for many through his powerful teaching, "Brave Communication." His strength in this area is part of the "secret sauce" that has helped Bethel's leadership be such an effective covenantal team over the years.

His most cherished gift and deepest joy is the life he shares with his wonderful wife, Christie, their flat-out amazing children Aiden, Macy, and Trace, and the good times they enjoy with extended family and friends.

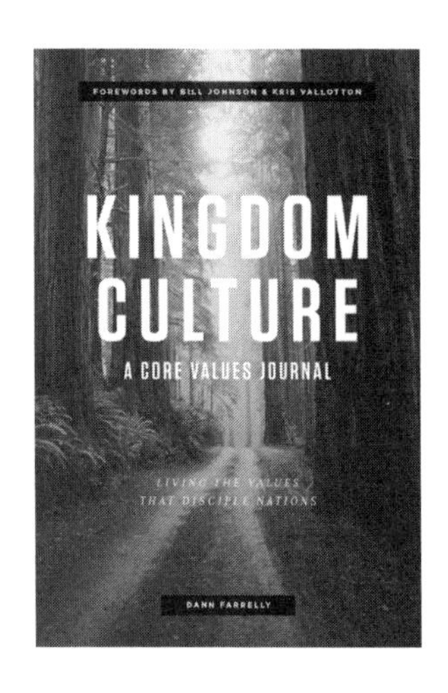

KINGDOM CULTURE

To find more information and resources on this topic please visit: *www.dannfarrelly.com*

To order additional copies of *Kingdom Culture*, please visit the Bethel Store at: *shop.bethel.com*

Are you interested in purchasing a quantity of books for your church, small group or staff? For discounts on bulk orders please contact us at: *info@dannfarrelly.com*

MORE RESOURCES FROM DANN

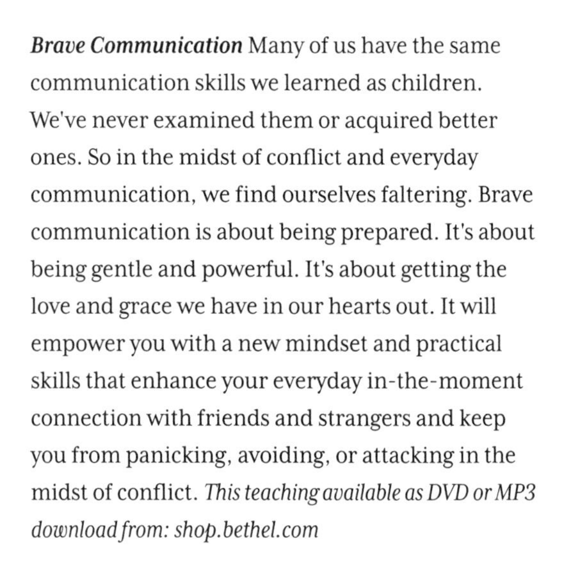

Brave Communication Many of us have the same communication skills we learned as children. We've never examined them or acquired better ones. So in the midst of conflict and everyday communication, we find ourselves faltering. Brave communication is about being prepared. It's about being gentle and powerful. It's about getting the love and grace we have in our hearts out. It will empower you with a new mindset and practical skills that enhance your everyday in-the-moment connection with friends and strangers and keep you from panicking, avoiding, or attacking in the midst of conflict. *This teaching available as DVD or MP3 download from: shop.bethel.com*